Endorsements for *No More Consultants* . . .

"The saying goes that consultants borrow your watch to tell you the time. This book is all about borrowing the consultant's watch. Practical, and rich with examples, it is about learning from and sharing good practices inside the organisation, and only looking outside for consultancy help where you really need it."

Graham O'Connell, Head of Organisational Learning
and Standards, National School of Government

"Look, of course we need outside input, if not we might as well be staring at our belly-buttons. The point that is being made in *No More Consultants* is that companies spend pennies in mining their own internal knowledge and expertise compared to the multi-millions spent on going outside first! How does that make any sense or cents?"

Jon Theuerkauf, Managing Director, Credit Suisse

"When facing a challenge, organizations need to know what capabilities they have, but it is not always easy to have honest conversations about who knows what. Here is a book that shows step by step how to help groups articulate what being good at something looks like – and then use this information to self-assess and get better. The authors have both a simple method and the wisdom of experience to make it come alive on complex issues. The result is an invaluable resource."

Etienne Wenger, author of Communities of Practice

"We have applied the innovative techniques described in *No More Consultants* to enable beneficiaries around the world to develop their capacity. Capacity development draws upon voluntary learning with genuine commitment and interest. The River Diagram and associated methodologies is a way to build on existing capacities, prompt knowledge sharing and optimize expertise."

Dr Carlos Lopes, UN Assistant-Secretary-General,
Executive Director of UNITAR and Director of the
United Nations System Staff College

"Consultants and smart clients: a rare and insightful view from both sides of the fence. Full of practical recommendations for achieving more value from both internal and external consultants and advisers."

Professor Edward Truch, Founder of the Henley
Knowledge Management Forum and Visiting Professor,
Lancaster University Management School

"The practical methodology – self-assessment framework – introduced by Chris Collison and Geoff Parcell with useful techniques and tips will enable many organizations to diagnose their own issues by themselves, and come up with their solutions, instead of relying on prescriptions by outsiders. The step-by-step guidance, and a full of diverse and real-life examples will help teams and organizations to develop their own self-assessment framework, open up the conversation among stakeholders, and improve the way they work."

Janice Ryu, Knowledge Management Officer,
International Finance Corporation, World Bank Group

"About time too! Following on from their excellent work in *Learning to Fly*, Geoff and Chris have come up with another practical yet powerful approach to help organisations get the most from what they already know. Successfully tried and tested in many different circumstances, their easy to follow advice puts the power to solve problems back into the hands of those who care most about the organisation and the outcome – those who need to live and work with the solution. An essential tool for anyone who has struggled to initiate change, implement a strategy or solve a problem with outside help, but found it slow going."

Professor Jane McKenzie, Henley Business School

"The best book by far on Knowledge Management is *Learning to Fly* by Chris Collison and Geoff Parcell. This new book is of equal calibre.

The authors are not theorists and this book is not only practical but is written in clear, simple language.

We have been taught to look to 'experts' for help and advice. And although we often do need guidance, we know more than we think. Given the complexity of our twenty-first century organizations it is dangerous to rely on external consultants who can never fully understand the richness of the context in which we work.

In this book, Chris and Geoff provide tools and techniques that allow us to tap into our innate capabilities and to do away with rather than automatically relying upon external consultants!"

David Gurteen, Founder and Director, Gurteen Knowledge Community

"By knowing what you know already and utilising the skills within your organisation, this book shows you how to kick the consultancy habit."

Michael Scott, Chief Executive, Westminster Primary Care Trust

"Simple, straightforward and eminently practical. Chris and Geoff have shown again the power of liberating the knowledge within and around any organisation."

John Keeble, Sales and Marketing Director, Aon Risk Services

"It's all about making connections and having the conversations – Geoff and Chris have provided great examples of what businesses can do on a practical, day to day basis to help improve performance and capability. Sharing and learning from each other – simple concepts that don't have to be wrapped up in complex, abstract processes."

Sindy Grewal, Head of Knowledge, Audit Commission

"Geoff and Chris have cooked up another winner – *No More Consultants*, is a brilliant, readable and most importantly, practical guide to unlocking a group's capacity to understand, improve and do their work. Heck, it isn't really about consultants at all, but our own power. Regardless if you are a business, a non profit or a community of practice, *No More Consultants* offers you a framework, tools and guidance. While I loved the whole book, here are some aspects I especially appreciated. It taps into strengths and assets of individuals and groups at every turn, from an appreciative approach to creating 'the river', to use of multiple intelligences in the processes put to use. It recognizes the importance of negotiating common language, self assessment (vs external) and the role of conversations to achieve this. I can't wait to put what I've learned to work. Tomorrow! Thanks Chris and Geoff!"

Nancy White, Founder, Full Circle Associates

"A misquote?: If it is dangerous to not know what you should know, then it can be disastrous for you to know something that is not so.

Mantra?: Perpetual learning is part of every managers/directors day job. You must never abdicate/delegate the thinking that you should do for yourself . . . or disaster beckons."

Peter Brickley, Group IT Director, Heineken

"Give an organisation a consultant, and solve today's problems.

Give an organisation tools to identify and use their existing skills and knowledge, to build networks to support knowledge sharing within and across organisations, and to help continuously improve these abilities, and you solve many of tomorrow's problems, without spending a fortune.

This book provides the tools – you just need to use them."

Helen Nicol, Internal Organisational Development Consultant, Department of Work and Pensions

"Once again Geoff and Chris inspire you to use simple tools and practices that can make a real difference to the knowledge ecology of the organisation and create the opportunity for sustained improvement."

Michael Norton, Improvement and Development Agency (IDeA)

"There is no shortage of knowledge and experience in local and regional government – the challenge is to find the best way to tap into it and get it flowing. In *No More Consultants*, Geoff and Chris show us how to overcome this challenge, and access and share the wealth of resources we already have available to us."

Keith Barnes, former Regional Director, Government Office for the North West

No More Consultants

We Know More Than We Think

Geoff Parcell & Chris Collison

WILEY

A John Wiley & Sons, Ltd., Publication

Front cover image protected by copyright, trademark, design and other rights of Tissot and shall not be copied or used or reproduced without prior written approval by Tissot.

Registered office
John Wiley & Sons Ltd, The Atrium, Southern Gate, Chichester, West Sussex, PO19 8SQ, United Kingdom

For details of our global editorial offices, for customer services and for information about how to apply for permission to reuse the copyright material in this book please see our website at www.wiley.com.

Library of Congress Cataloging-in-Publication Data

Collison, Chris.
  No more consultants : we know more than we think / Chris Collison, Geoff Parcell.
     p. cm.
  Includes bibliographical references and index.
  ISBN 978-0-470-74603-5 (hardback)
  1. Knowledge management. 2. Organizational learning. I. Parcell, Geoff.
II. Title.
  HD30.2.C6284 2009
  658.4′038—dc22
                                                                   2009027973
A catalogue record for this book is available from the British Library.

Set in 11/14 pt Trebuchet MS by SNP Best-set Typesetter Ltd., Hong Kong
Printed in Great Britain by TJ International Ltd, Padstow, Cornwall, UK

This book is dedicated

to all those who have helped us learn,

and to all those who will continue

to do so in the future.

Contents

Foreword

Morpheus: 'I imagine that right now, you're feeling a bit like Alice. Hmm? Tumbling down the rabbit hole? ... You take the blue pill, the story ends. You wake up in your bed and believe whatever you want to believe. You take the red pill, you stay in wonderland. And I show you how deep the rabbit hole goes.' – *The Matrix*

Geoff Parcell and Chris Collison have designed the perfect red pill ... showing you all the secrets of consulting's wonderland and rabbit holes, with no bad side-effects.

In today's fast-paced and crazed world, we're so often forced into the quick fix that consultants can provide, we forget that the only true solutions come from a Zen-like focus on big questions: What problem am I trying to solve? What do I know and not know about how to solve it? Am I willing to live with the questions long enough to allow the answers to reveal themselves?

Like Zen masters, Geoff and Chris begin our journey with questions such as these. *No More Consultants* is a tool for answering the five core questions that will help you eliminate, reduce and focus your use of consultants, and when you do use them, get the most value for the least effort and lowest cost.

From my life's work, I would say the most critical of their five questions is *Can we identify the issue*? I have found that almost all clients are trying to solve the wrong problem. And that's a consultant's dream! You're either guaranteeing them a retainer for life, or that you'll pay them lots of money to keep solving the wrong problems, until eventually you stumble upon the real one. The good news is that if you follow what Geoff and Chris have laid out, that won't happen to you!

Major takeaways:

- You can be more purposeful in your use of consultants if you understand the problem well enough to seek help within the organisation before going out to consultants.

- By consistently looking inside first, you unleash the untapped energy and strengths of the organisation.

Years ago, I was brought in by one of the world's largest banks to simplify and communicate a massive change they were about to roll out within their compensation plan. The change was called broadbanding, where the company would shift from about thirty pay grades to only about seven. Fortunately, I had one of those clients who allowed me to ask the right questions, and discover what the real problem was. And it had nothing to do with compensation!

The hidden challenge that revealed itself was budgeting. See, making this shift meant that someone whose pay grade only allowed a $2000 top-to-bottom swing, would now have a $10000+ top-to-bottom swing. The senior execs in charge of budgets were freaked out! They thought that meant that they'd completely lose all control of their human resource costs – which was the largest line item in their budgets.

The problem I was originally brought in to solve was how to get 70000 people to understand how their pay would remain the same, but their pay grade would change. We discovered that was a secondary problem for later. The more urgent one was to help fifty executives understand how to do budgeting within a broadbanded world. Completely different problem that required a completely approach, solution, scale and urgency.

The result of that one day of asking the right questions: The client didn't need me any further! *No more consultant*! (At least not for another six months, and by then, the scope of the project had been greatly reduced.) What happened by the end of that meeting is what Geoff and Chris call *Finding the River*: Once we clarified what the real problem was, the client could quickly figure out that most of what he needed to solve the new problem was already sitting within his organisation!

Fast forward through the rest of this awesome book to its close. Geoff and Chris end with '... You know more than you think.' You do! Just like in the *Matrix*, when Trinity says to Neo, 'The answer is out there ... it's looking for you, and you will find it if you want to.'

Everything you need to know about no more consultants is within *No More Consultants*. It helps you tap into your power of self-assessment. Let the answer reveal itself to you, and enjoy the journey!

Bill Jensen, Mr Simplicity
author of *Simplicity: The New Competitive Advantage* and other books, all about finding what matters within all the noise and clutter.

Preface

I n 2001, we wrote our first book together – *Learning to Fly*. At that time, we were both working for BP, the energy company and wanted to share our experience and learning from a successful knowledge-sharing programme. Three years later, we wrote the second edition: *Learning to Fly – Practical Knowledge Management from Leading and Learning Organizations*, which incorporated the experience of many other others in the public, private and development sectors, using a number of tools and techniques to help knowledge flow around and between organisations. Since that time, we have been practising what we know – and, as independent consultants and advisors, working in many more different contexts, learning a lot more.

I guess we have all smiled wryly at the author Robert Townsend's well-known quote: 'Consultants ask to borrow your watch to tell you the time, and then walk off with your watch!' Whilst we smile though, we know that there is an element of truth in the quote.

During our roles in multinational organisations, we have been on the receiving end of recommendations offered by external management consultants. We have both had roles in those same organisations as internal consultants; and over the past four years, we have also experienced being hired as external consultants. From these various viewpoints we have observed that consultants are not always hired for the right reasons and are frequently not deployed to optimum effect.

No More Consultants is a book which raises the question of how we can be more *purposeful* in our use of management consultants. It is a book for managers who commission consultants to help deliver their business results. It is also a book for the people within organisations who feel that they have the knowledge and capability themselves to solve some of the issues that highly paid consultants are brought in to address – leaving their recommendations for others to implement. *No More Consultants* is the book you'd buy for someone who is committed to continuous improvement, and is frustrated that their organisation unthinkingly relies too much on external help.

We believe organisations can do more to learn what, and where, their strengths are in order to first benefit from their own good practices. We have used the self-assessment approach described in the book in many settings and for a number of topics. From our experience, we know that this approach is transferable. We will explain in detail how to determine and make best possible use of what your organisation already knows. This in turn will help you to establish whether and when to bring in consultants so that you get the best from what they have to offer you.

There are many people to acknowledge who helped in the writing of this book but in particular, we want to thank:

Sophie Smiles Director of i&i

Graham O'Connell, Head of Organisational Development at the National School of Government

Karen Eden, Director, EMEA Partnering Excellence Programme Office, Oracle

Deborah Pilkington at the Government Office of the NW

Lynne Keech, Knowledge Consultant at Nationwide

The coaches at the Constellation for AIDS Competence

Rachel Cooke, research fellow at the NHS Institute for Improvement and Innovation

Professor Vicharn Panich of the Knowledge Management Institute in Thailand

Professor Martin Elliott at Great Ormond Street Hospital, (and Ferrari)

Charlotte Diez at UNITAR

Phil Forth and Barry Smale for painstakingly reading and editing the proofs.

And of course, our wives and families for their enduring support and encouragement – again!

Geoff Parcell & Chris Collison
August 2009

Introduction – Why *No More Consultants*?

From time to time, most organisations bring in teams of consultants; perhaps to help develop strategies, advise on policies or solve thorny problems. Your organisation might be planning to move to the next level of performance, and need some inspiration from outside. It could be that you believe that you need professional assistance in introducing change: a new enterprise software platform, a new strategy, evaluating new business opportunities, outsourcing or off-shoring. Consultants are also brought into organisations to help deal with something unexpected; a financial downturn, an opportunistic acquisition or disposal, or the succession of a senior executive.

Why is it that so often the instinctive response to such changes, planned or unplanned, is to employ consulting resources from outside the organisation?

Sometimes we need a neutral agent to disentangle the emotion and politics from hard-nosed business decisions.

Sometimes, the personal stakes are high, and we feel we really don't want to get this wrong.

Sometimes our own internal staff are too busy doing the day-to-day work, so we need to buy in temporary extra capacity.

Sometimes it seems the external consultant's voice carries more weight with senior management, or is considered to be impartial.

Sometimes they are expected to make unpalatable recommendations and it will be cathartic to be able to blame them for the decision (and also if things go wrong!).

Sometimes, however, we just press the consultancy button without really thinking it through. That's not smart.

So the consultants arrive, interview the stakeholders, diagnose the problem and formulate some recommendations. Their recommendations are often afforded a level of respect by the management team, a level which would never be offered to suggestions which came directly from the employees. As a consequence, members of staff are left with a frustration that the consultants drew all of the ideas, solutions and expertise from within the organisation, yet they took all the credit for the recommendations themselves.

Having delivered their finely crafted PowerPoint presentation, the consultancy team exits the stage, leaving behind a set of strategies or solutions to be implemented.

Unfortunately, the staff who are tasked with implementation don't feel that they 'own' the solutions, and the results often fall far short of the PowerPoint dreams from the boardroom.

'Perhaps we need to bring in some trouble-shooters to help us understand why the implementation failed? Now where's that business card that someone gave me ...?'

Stop! Please stop!

Since we left major organisations and became independent consultants we have learned a lot by working with a variety of different groups and organisations. In particular, we have learned that a self-assessment approach is a highly effective way of having the right conversations. The right conversations are the ones which lead you to discover the knowledge and experience which is most important to the organisation, and the actions it needs to take in order to be successful.

Five Key Questions

We believe that there are five key questions for an organisation to pose:

- Can we identify the issue?

- Do we know our internal capability?

- Does anyone do this well internally?

- Do we know who is good at it externally?

- Having identified who does it well, are they available to help us, either by sharing what they know or by implementing it?

Let's explore each of these questions in more detail.

Can We Identify the Issue?

One of the biggest challenges facing an organisation that is striving to improve its performance is to identify the right issue to tackle. Much valuable time and resource can be wasted by people solving the wrong issue. In our experience, the person posing the question 'What's the real issue here?' will get a different response depending on whether the respondent has the title of IT consultant, Business Manager, HR professional or Senior Engineer. If you have a tool in your hand when you pose the question, this will inevitably frame the way you define the issue too. When all you have is a hammer, everything looks like a nail! But if the real issue was hanging a picture to maximise its impact, then perhaps you should have been considering if the picture was right for the style and colour scheme of the room long before you reached for the wall-fixings.

There have been many instances where lack of diagnosis of the issue has led to a lot of wasted effort in resolving the wrong issue. Time spent analysing the underlying issue is well spent to ensure that the solutions considered address the right issue. Sometimes this can be more obvious to a pair of 'outside eyes', that is, people not too close to the issue and who have the benefit of other contexts. Are you recognising the symptoms and dealing with those or diagnosing the root cause? After all, it is more effective to do the right thing than do things right.

Do We Know Our Internal Capability?

Donald Rumsfeld the US Defense Secretary is quoted as saying:

> I don't know what the facts are but somebody's certainly going to sit down with him and find out what he knows that they may not know, and make sure he knows what they know that he may not know.

Now I don't know if I know what I think he wanted to say ... but many organisations simply do not know what they know.

As individuals, we are usually known for the work we are currently doing, and even if our résumé is up to date and available for others to read, it probably does not describe what we know, merely what our past positions were or what we have done.

Once you have the issue clear, ask yourself 'do you know if anyone is already doing this in-house?'. The emphasis here is on the *knowing* because frequently we do not know what the organisation knows. If someone does know and has experience of doing it, we can then check if they do it well and if they are available to help us. If we do not know whether or not we have good practice in-house – and in our experience this is most often the case – then finding out if the knowledge exists in other departments or project groups is a good first step. If you do have a way of finding out that the knowledge exists then getting together to share that knowledge may be all that is required to tackle the issue yourselves. In previous books, we have written about bespoke 'yellow pages systems' to share who we are, what we know and what we are prepared to share. In today's Web 2.0 world we can use any number of social networking sites to achieve the same end. It's often easier to discover the abilities and experience of your work colleagues through LinkedIn, Facebook or Xing, than it is to use the formal corporate systems.

Does Anyone Do this Well Internally?

Find out who does it well, where the strengths lie in the organisation. Too often we look only at the current competencies being used and are ignorant of what additional strengths people have that are also available to the organisation. It is possible that all the knowledge and resources you need may be there, but since this is not a business-as-usual activity, it can be worth having a coach help the team get to 'match fitness'.

For example, in any change programme it is common to assemble a task force from those in the organisation who are likely to have to live through the change and to make it happen. One reason for doing this is to ensure ownership of the solution; there is nothing worse than feeling that you are having change imposed upon you. This task force team might comprise a wide range of people, levels and roles. A temporary project team such as this, which includes accountants, engineers or nurses, may or may not feel confident to facilitate brainstorming sessions or draw process flow diagrams. Their diversity is positive when it comes to understanding the issue but it may need harnessing.

Do We Know Who is Good at it Externally?

If we know that we don't have the capability in-house, then who does possess the key knowledge that we could reach out to? By extending our social networks further, we might identify and be able to approach 'people who know' in other organisations. If you are not competing directly with the organisation, or if the issue is not commercially sensitive – Health and Safety for instance – then people are normally receptive to requests to share good practice. People feel appreciated for their strengths, and it gives them a sense of pride to be helping others.

Are the People with the Knowledge Available to Help Us?

We may have the capability and know-how, or have learned it from others, yet because of competing priorities, a matter of timing or a surfeit of initiatives from HQ, we need additional people to help deliver a solution. Here the politics of hierarchical organisations can prove a barrier. Different parts of the organisation and different managers have their own objectives and priorities and may feel possessive about the resources they control.

Do we need to hire staff on a permanent basis or do we just want to outsource this particular task? In a cost-conscious, competitive world it does not make sense to maintain staff levels for all eventualities but rather to err on the lean side and recruit short-term labour with the relevant skills to manage the peaks of work. Conversely, you might perceive an ongoing need and take steps to recruit people with the right skills and knowledge.

If the knowledge lies outside the organisation will they be prepared to assist us? Do we have an existing relationship? Is there something we can offer that they need, to reciprocate the help? Or is this a conversation we can both benefit from?

How to Read *No More Consultants*

People are often looking for the proverbial 'low hanging fruits' – the quick wins to achieve a marked improvement in performance without a big initiative or extra resources. In the book we explain in detail an approach which covers identifying an issue, generating ownership of that issue, developing a self-assessment tool and using it to identify strengths, a way of visualising different strengths in different parts of the organisation, and how to learn from others. The approach helps people to focus their sharing and learning on the practices which are already proven to work elsewhere in the organisation, or in other organisations. In short, it helps you accelerate around the learning cycle.

If you want to tap into what is already known in order to resolve your big issues then this book is for you.

The approach will enable you to take an overview of the current capability of the organisation and identify the variations across it. To raise the overall capability levels, you need to get the right people sharing their expertise with those who are keen to learn. This book contains step-by-step guidance, and a number of powerful examples to inspire you.

Perhaps you are looking for the key practices, need some external focus or support in order to improve? You want to know exactly where to target training, mentoring or new ideas from other organisations but you can't be certain that you're shining the spotlight in the right places. Maybe you have been challenged to demonstrate progress in improvement and want a way to measure the increase in capability over time, highlighting where improvements have been made, and where they need to be made.

If you have mentally, or physically, nodded through any of the above, then as you read through the book, have a topic in mind. Is there a topic or capability which your organisation needs to develop or improve in order to perform better?

As we go through the book we are going to introduce you to a number of illustrative stories – real practical examples – from a number of sectors.

In BP, a top-down directive was to focus on Operations excellence, improving the operational capability of more than 800 separate operational sites and pursuing an improvement prize worth in excess of $400 million.

Nine regional government offices in the UK learned where their strengths in knowledge management were and how to build capability in those practices where they were weak.

Nationwide Building Society developed its Supply chain to make sure the links of the whole chain were supporting one another.

The National Health Service (NHS) is developing a knowledge culture. Staff at Great Ormond Street hospital recognised that one of the most vulnerable times was in transferring sick babies or children from the operating theatre to the intensive care ward.

In Thailand, the Khao Kwan Foundation is helping rice farmers to shift to organic farming methods.

At Oracle they are strengthening their international professional communities so that they contribute to the company's goals.

OneSixSigma is a cross-industry consortium of business improvement experts, extending its area of interest beyond Six Sigma to find new, additional topics around which they could connect and discuss. But how could they find the right topics to maximise the potential of the group?

The United Nations' UNAIDS organisation identifies good practice but was challenged to effectively share globally the local responses to AIDS as their big issue. This challenge has been taken up by the Constellation for AIDS Competence who are now working to reveal strengths and connect local responses around the world.

The UK's National School for Government realised they could improve their Learning & Development capacity by sharing across the network.

The United Nation Institute for Training and Research (UNITAR) has a Decentralised Cooperation programme which connects cities around the world to learn from each other and share their strengths.

We hope that aspects of each of these stories will help you identify the needs of your organisation, and inspire you deal with them.

This book will give you all you need to build a common framework and language to allow sharing to take place. In turn, this framework will enable different groups to self-assess and discuss their collective competence and share experience; what works and what doesn't. People can identify their current strengths and prioritise areas to improve, sharing the improvement and the learning with others in the organisation. When the same groups repeat the exercise six months or a year later, they have a measure of how effective they have been at building up their capability.

As you read through the chapters try to suspend your search for comparisons; 'Isn't this just like balanced scorecards?', or 'APQC have a self-assessment questionnaire' or 'This is Appreciative Inquiry'. There are some common elements, but there are also some significant differences which you may miss if you put it in the same 'pigeonhole' as another method. Suspend evaluation and learn afresh. You can make comparisons later and adapt the approach we are sharing to your own needs.

The following chapters will take you through the context and the steps required to identify the practices which are important, engaging a group to help define the levels of competence, having a conversation to determine current and desired levels and identifying how to get to your desired level. We also explain how to revisit the self-assessment framework, firstly to improve to the next level and then to amend the framework to keep you striving for improvement. We'll show you some creative and innovative ways of looking at the performance information to help anyone in your organisation to readily identify who they can share your strengths with and in return, who they can learn from to improve.

Chapter by Chapter

Here's what you can expect to find in each chapter:

Chapter 2 – Finding the River

This is the introduction to the approach which will enable you to recognise and harness the capability that already exists somewhere inside your organisation, in order to reach your objectives. We'll explore why this is relevant, what the next steps are to help you achieve what your dream of success looks like, which tools and resources are available and how you might apply it in your own organisation or community.

The common language that a self-assessment framework provides is very effective in identifying opportunities for learning and sharing, but if a picture is worth a thousand words, how can this huge improvement potential be visualised and communicated in a memorable way? The 'River Diagram' provides this perspective, and has become a powerful metaphor. This chapter introduces the River Diagram, and explains how to use it to start a knowledge-sharing revolution. It will help you examine the distribution of performance across your organisation, and if you watch the river over time you can track the improvement in performance.

Chapter 3 – Building the Framework

This chapter takes you through building your own self-assessment framework. The self-assessment framework is the key tool in this approach, because it provides both the breadth of the topic and the common language which you can use to share experience. However, this is not an end in itself. We have all had the experience of discussing something familiar using common words and phrases only to learn afterwards that we were talking about something different. I recently launched into a conversation about 'networks' only to discover that the other person was talking about the wires and routers that link computers, whilst I was talking about people connected by a common interest.

Perhaps you've discussed an issue with someone in a different department and they have assured you 'Oh yes, I already have that covered', only to discover later that what they were referring to was only a portion of what you had in mind – you didn't both share the same view of the bigger picture. The role that the self-assessment framework plays is to agree on the language so that knowledge can be shared easily. The framework contains a number of practices and five levels of competence for each practice. The framework is designed to create the right conversations and also to encourage ownership of the problem and solution. Consequently, the approach takes communities and organisations from a victim mindset, to owning both the issue and the response to it. The resulting actions are dependent on the diversity of people involved in the conversation.

Chapter 4 – Applying the Approach

We have a choice. We can choose to focus on what works or we can look for what doesn't work. Whatever we look for is what we are likely to find! That's the essence of Positive Deviance; all too often we choose to view the world as problems to solve, and quite often we find that we chose to solve the wrong problem!

This chapter explains how the approach shifts the paradigm from making an intervention to solve someone else's problem (and in the process making that someone else the victim) to facilitating a group to identify their own strengths and support them to build on these to arrive at their own solutions. Experiences are shared and compared with the words in the framework to ensure that the breadth of the practices is covered. Together the participants can then decide how to adapt those experiences to their own situations. The power of the approach is in the ownership it engenders through conversation.

Chapter 5 – The Role of the Facilitator

Facilitation is essential to ensure that the space exists for people to learn from one another and to build common understanding and expertise. We look at the role of a facilitator from first principles, and help you to define this important activity. Facilitation is key to enabling the free flow of knowledge.

Chapter 6 – Creating the River

Having introduced the concept of the River Diagram earlier in the book, this chapter looks at the details of how you build and use your own version of the river, and how you take others with you on the journey. We look at several practical ways to create a River Diagram for different audiences, using a variety of media and locations; flipchart paper, Microsoft Excel, in a village square and on a houseboat on a river in Kerala, India.

This is performance improvement with a difference!

Chapter 7 – Learning from Experience

Creating a self-assessment framework and presenting the results visually can stimulate an organisation into action, but just knowing that there is someone with whom you can share – or someone that you can learn from – is often insufficient. By bringing together those with strengths to share and those with something to learn, a tremendous amount of sharing can take place, based on real experiences. However, the apparently simple logic of connecting sharers with learners (balancing supply with demand) can become derailed with the reality of human behaviour. Pride, reticence, a desire to invent and political self-sufficiency and are just some of the behavioural barriers which are erected against the flow of learning. We investigate some of barriers to sharing and suggest practical steps to overcome them, and keep the momentum building.

Chapter 8 – Improving and Sustaining

There is nothing magical about the selection of practices and levels, other than that they are agreed upon by people with access to expertise and experience of applying that expertise. Perhaps after having used the framework for a year, you decide that other practices are more relevant, or good practices have pushed the boundaries of competence to a higher level. This is what continuous improvement is all about. A balance must be struck between improving the framework and the ability to compare and measure progress. This process is all about continuous improvement; having a framework to check your current capabilities and a process to improve. By repeating the process after an interval, it is possible to measure progress and create momentum such that, over time, this becomes the way of working.

Chapter 9 – So What Do We Do Now?

Are we really suggesting that consultants are not needed?

No, we are not. However, we can be more purposeful in whom we select, and why and when we bring them into our organisations.

By the time you get to the end of the book you'll be feeling confident to run a meeting to set up a self-assessment approach and you will know how to take it forward. You'll understand how to use a structured process for engaging your organisation in dialogue about the relative strengths and weaknesses and the variations across the organisation, without egos and competition getting in the way.

This final chapter revisits the role of consultants and with the help of a simple flow-chart, helps you validate your decisions at each stage.

Following the flow-chart will ensure that you get best use and best value from what you know – and from the added value that consultants, when used appropriately, will bring.

You know more than you think. We want to help you to think more about what you know.

Discovering the River

2

Think of a river. It's springtime. Imagine that you are taking a relaxing country walk beside the river. As you amble along the edge of one of the banks, you begin to notice its characteristics. The ground where you are walking is well-trodden – much of the grass has been worn away by the trampling feet of armies of fellow travellers, leaving a hardened brown path. As you peer over the edge of the bank, the water nearest you is moving slowly over the river bed, occasionally interrupted by patches of pebbles and silt. A little further down, low-hanging tree branches have snagged a discarded plastic bag, which in turn attracts more flotsam, mostly twigs and leaves, as the river continues on its journey. You stoop and settle down on the edge of the river, your legs dangling over the low bank and your eyes rest upon a leaf in the water nearby. You become entranced as it repeats an endless waltz, caught in a small eddy current which returns it time and again to whence it started. Will it free itself this time and join the faster current further out? The leaf dances and drift right to the point of escape ... only to be recaptured by the eddy and returning to the margin of the river with the resigned helplessness of a habitual re-offender.

Picking up a stone, you throw it further out. It falls with a satisfyingly deep 'plop' which tells you that the water there is deeper. Looking up and out, you can see that nearer to the other bank, the water runs faster and clearer. The banks are sheer, clearly defined by the faster currents. The grass beyond is lush and unspoiled. You throw another stone, and another. Each one disappears into the fast-flowing current; no ripples, no trace. Searching on the ground, you find a rounded pebble. You get to your feet to hurl it towards the far side with all your strength – will it still fall short of the bank? Can it be reached from here?

Does any of this sound familiar? How often do we find inspirational business performance in organisations where staff feel like the leaf caught in a circulating current? Can you recognise the patches of silt and pebbles which impede the flow of value? Has the fast current of the organisation swept away the stones of individual efforts?

Compare this attempt to reach the other side of the river with the oft repeated mantra – 'Seek out and apply best practice.' Journals, books and management consultants line up to explain why their 'best practice' is really the best – rather than just 'good' or merely 'different'.

Despite the mantra and claims, your years of experience tell you that that the grass really is greener on the other side; it's just reaching the other side which presents the challenge. Those stepping stones which appear to take you there are not as helpful as you thought and often turn out to be partly submerged alligators!

So how do we cross the river to find the faster flowing deeper, clear water which represents outstanding performance? Stay put, standing there on the bank, pebble in hand – we'll be back ...

In this chapter we will show you how to find the rivers in your organisation, and more importantly, how to help your organisation to chart and navigate them.

We will start by looking at how to know what your organisation knows, to introduce an approach which will enable people to recognise and harness the capability that already exists, in order to reach their objectives. The approach is all about creating the right conversations to identify strengths and to choose where to build capability and capacity, and where to buy it in. Having identified the strengths and sources of capability, the next step is to share this capability across the organisation.

Whilst there are a number of capability assessment and analysis approaches available to organisations, one of the things that makes this approach special is that a group can self-assess its own strengths and build on these by sharing with other departments or teams having different strengths. This process of self-assessment empowers the group to take its own actions.

The self-assessment framework which makes this possible defines both the breadth and the boundaries for the conversation. The framework also provides a common language that enables learning and sharing, and we will cover this in detail in the next chapter. If the self-assessment provides the breadth and the boundaries, then there is one additional step necessary to bring the results to life in a visual and innovative way.

It is often said that a picture is worth a thousand words. Imagine then the value of a picture that illustrates at a glance how a company's operations are performing. This can be worth millions of dollars. The 'River Diagram' provides this perspective, and Chapter 6 explains how to create and use a River Diagram, how it can bring about the start of a knowledge-sharing revolution.

BP produced such a picture from a common set of self-assessment measures, relevant to all of their hundred business operations worldwide, whether drilling, refining or manufacturing chemicals.

For now, think of it as a simple 'health check' matrix – the kind of tool that consultants often bring into organisations – but this one was built by the BP staff themselves. We described this in a previous book, *Learning to Fly*, and since this is where the approach began, it is worth repeating.

Every business unit used it to score their performance for a number of practices, on a scale of one to five, where five represented world-class performance and one equated to basic performance (Figure 2.1).

Practice 1	Practice 2	Practice 3	Practice 4	Practice 5
5				
4				
3				
2				
1				

Figure 2.1 Self-assessment matrix.

In BP's 'Operational Excellence' self-assessment, the practices included such topics as 'Manage corrosion', 'Manage third parties and contractors', 'Manage greenhouse gas emissions' and 'Communicate effectively': 25 practices in total. Every business unit scored themselves against each of the 25 practices, asking 'Which level are we currently at – which set of words in the self-assessment matrix describes us best?' and then set improvement targets for a smaller number (around 20%) of practices – the ones which were the business priorities.

Forming the River

BP's 'worth a thousand words' picture portrayed the range of scores against all of the practice areas that had

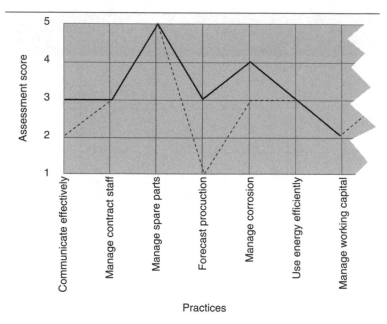

Figure 2.2 Performance chart.

been defined, and could be used as a backdrop against which any single business could measure itself.

Similar to the self-assessment matrix, the diagram has as a vertical axis from level one (basic performance) to five (world-class performance). The horizontal axis lists the various practices, side by side (Figure 2.2).

Having completed their self-assessment, any business can see its current performance scores laid out against this framework – a unique, meandering line which represents their performance.

When their target scores are overlaid on this chart, the gaps between current performance and target perform-

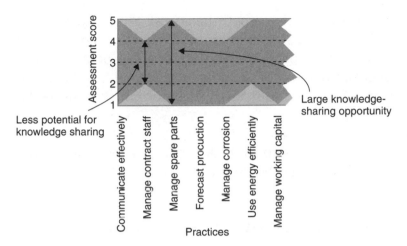

Figure 2.3 River Diagram.

ance become very clear, providing the managers of that business with some areas to focus on.

When the scores were aggregated for all businesses, some common trends emerged. For example, not one of the hundred operational businesses reported world-class (level five) performance in the areas entitled 'Forecast production' and 'Manage corrosion'. Conversely, no businesses reported basic performance in the areas of 'Manage contract staff' or 'Use energy efficiently'. A single picture was created which aggregated all the individual scores to illustrate these trends (Figure 2.3).

This picture was to become known, company-wide as the 'River Diagram': the boundaries of the river represent the maximum and minimum scores that any business has reported, so the river represents a spread or range of scores. The 'banks' of the river are those areas mentioned earlier, where no businesses has recorded a score.

The presence of a 'south bank', at the bottom of the diagram, indicated a reasonable level of competence inside the company (everyone at level two or above). The presence of a 'north bank' (no one at level five) indicated where BP lacked sufficiently high performance inside the company.

Let's take a minute to think about how the shape of the north bank might be useful.

Beating Consultants at Their Own Game

When I worked in major corporations as an employee, one of the most frequently voiced complaints that I would hear about external consultants is that they charge extortionate rates to tell you what you already know.

Having said that, wouldn't it be powerful to be able to better focus the power of an external consultant on precisely the areas where they can add real value? After all, if you have examples of great performance within the company, you can improve dramatically by simply learning from those first – charity begins at home, right?

This is where the River Diagram is particularly useful. The north bank of the river shows you where nobody within the organization has a high level of capability; this is where an external view can add value by providing the examples and support necessary to help fill your knowledge gap. Where no north bank exists, you already have the capability somewhere inside your organization – the potential is there, perhaps not evenly distributed and

just needing to be released. Send the external consultants packing and focus on your task – to identify the good
practices, get the right people talking and hence lever-
age the value.

Spotting the Potential for Learning and Sharing

In addition to the shape of the banks, there is another
highly valuable insight to be drawn from a River Diagram
– one which has great relevance to anyone charged with
the sharing of knowledge and good practices. The width
of the river at any single point gives a clear indication of
the potential for sharing and learning. Where BP's river
was narrow ('Manage contract staff', in Figure 2.3), most
businesses were of similar performance, and no real
breakthroughs had been identified internally. Where the
river was widest ('Manage spare parts'), this indicated
that a wide mix of performance, tremendous opportunities for sharing and improving performance existed.

Whilst we were working with BP's operational excellence
programme, we were particularly interested in the wide
points of the river because suddenly staring us in the face
was a picture that showed us where to focus knowledge-
sharing activities. We encouraged and supported internal
conferences, 'Peer Assist' workshops and the consolida-
tion of good practice examples and stories into 'knowledge assets' on these topics.

People often talk about 'low hanging fruits' – the River
Diagram actually shows you where they are growing –
where the river is at its widest!

The River Diagrams proved to be a popular and non-threatening way to think about performance relative to the company as a whole. It would tell an operations manager how strong or weak their performance was relative to all others.

The non-threatening nature of the River Diagram turned out to be a key characteristic. Rather than creating a league table of standings, which throws a harsh spotlight on 'who is best and who is worst overall', the River Diagram reveals the best that everyone can offer, their particular strengths. League tables can create defensiveness and reinforce a 'knowledge is power' culture. By contrast, River Diagrams illustrate the opportunities for learning and improving.

A second characteristic of River Diagrams is that the metaphor seems to work well at any level in the organisation – everyone can relate to the idea of a river. Senior managers like it because it rises above the complexity of the data and gives strategic insight. People at the frontline like it because it shows them where they can find help in the organisation.

Examining the Distribution of Performance

If you put yourself in the shoes of an operations manager who has completed his self-assessment, and committed to make an improvement in one of the practices – let's say, 'Using energy efficiently', the River Diagram is interesting, but doesn't answer the question 'Who can I learn from?' What they really want to do is dive into the river and see the distribution of scores across different business units. We liked the idea of diving into the river, but struggled to find the 'dive in' function in Excel! Instead, we generated a second view for which the y axis was also performance (on a one to five scale), but the x axis was the size of the gap between current performance, and the target score. The target score is the desired level for an agreed time period, say two years. You could say that the x axis was therefore a measure of the desire to improve (Figure 2.4).

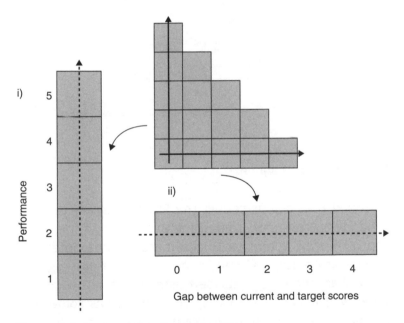

Figure 2.4 Constructing the Stairs Diagram.

In the example, which follows, business unit A has level four performance, and wants to improve by one level. Business unit B has level one performance, but wants to improve by three levels (perhaps a little ambitious, depending on the timescale). Finally, business unit C has level two performance, but has recorded no improvement target for this practice. They have selected other priorities to start on – after all, they can't realistically improve everything at once.

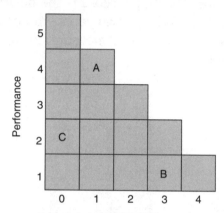

Figure 2.5 Stairs Diagram.

BP found that colour-coding the Stairs Diagram to highlight the extremes of 'something to share' and 'desire to improve' drew attention to the matchmaking potential. So once an operational unit, or a department or a regional office has completed its self-assessment, it wants to know who it can learn from, and who it has something to share with. The Stairs Diagram illustrates this for each practice. Story 2 in Chapter 3 demonstrates the use of both the River Diagram and the Stairs Diagram.

If you step back into the shoes of that operations manager, there are perhaps two questions that you might be asking.

Firstly, who can I learn from? Who can show me what good practice looks like in real life, and give me some pointers on how to apply it in my own business? Secondly, who can I learn with? Who is like me, at a similar level of performance, and wants to improve. Perhaps we can buddy-up and learn together?

This second question becomes important when there is just one high-performing business unit, who can find themselves on the receiving end of a large number of telephone calls, e-mails and visits. Cynics in BP used the term 'industrial tourism' to describe this phenomenon. It was better in the cases of these 'outliers' to coordinate activity between the business units wanting to learn – to hold a video or web-conference, a face-to-face meeting or 'Peer Assist', or to help them to capture their story electronically to share with a wider audience.

Watching the River Over Time

I used to live opposite a large bend in the River Thames and grew used to the sight of keen anglers camping out on the grassy bank opposite. Some of them seemed to be there permanently, studying the water for signs of sub-surface interest for what seemed like days, but I never saw them catch anything. I've always had my suspicions that anglers are solitary creatures and are looking for an excuse to stay out of their homes ...

However, observing a River Diagram over time can provide a valuable catch for an organisation. If you are able to repeat the self-assessment process at regular intervals

– say every 6-12 months, depending on the subject area, you can build up a profile of the changes in capability over time. You might even get creative and produce an animation which shows how the river is migrating.

Learning organisations will be able to demonstrate that the width of the river is narrowing in the areas of greatest value. Organisations with effective external benchmarking activity will demonstrate this by 'eroding away the north bank'.

Organisations with successful improvement and deployment programmes will see themselves 'depositing sediment' on the south bank, as more and more groups move out of the areas of low capability.

Thinking about the shape of the river that you would like to see in your organisation over a number of years can be a powerful way to develop an improvement strategy. Where does the greatest value lie – in eroding the north bank or escaping the south bank? Which areas would we like to see improving across all parts of our business? Do we need to put in place any interventions to accelerate this, or is there already sufficient sharing and learning?

We created a process to encourage common measures and the sharing of good practices across all of BP's operational sites. Having a common language and a common self-assessment tool for all operations is tremendously powerful and enabled sharing between previously unrelated businesses. We also coached the senior management to ask questions such as, 'Who have you talked to in order to improve your operational performance?' However, senior management needed to be coached too.

'Just tell me which business unit is the lowest overall ...'

We consciously resisted the request to sum the scores across the practices to get an absolute score for a refinery or a chemical factory. We weren't interested in absolute comparison – that would take us back to the world of league tables, and the negative behaviours which they can generate. By measuring and showing the scores spread out along the river bank, we were deliberately sharing the details on a practice-by-practice basis, rather than as an aggregate. We asserted that everybody is good at something, hence there were always some positive messages for each business. At a BP operations conference, a senior manager stated:

> We have world class performance in almost every single practice – somewhere within the company. The trick is to recognise where it lies, and to apply it globally.

That same manager might not have been at all receptive to an abstract conversation about 'managing knowledge', but in the context of the opportunity for business improvement, knowledge-sharing came to life for him.

In the next chapter, we'll look in detail at the self-assessment framework, and the steps necessary to build it. We'll leave the oil industry behind, and see how self-assessment created ripples in many pools – from the UK government to a mutual bank and a cross-industry business improvement consortium.

Bring that pebble with you!

Building the Framework

3

The self-assessment framework is the key tool in this approach; it's the tool which provides you with a description of what 'good' looks like, and a common language. However, it should not be viewed as an end in itself. Always bear in mind that the framework exists to create the right conversations, to recognise existing strengths and to encourage ownership of the problem (or gap in performance) and the solution. The approach is designed to take organisations and communities out of feeling like the victim to a state where they are confidently controlling their destiny. This is the reason that we emphasise the use of self-assessment, rather than inspection or audit. Self-assessment unleashes the latent power of an organisation or community.

The role of the framework is to agree on the language so that knowledge can be shared easily. The *practices* define the breadth of the topic, and are designed to ensure that all important aspects of the topic are considered. The *levels* define the depth of knowledge about the practices. In effect the level five of all practices defines the strategic intent, as it describes what great performance, or best-in-class capability looks like. The direction of the conversation, and the actions that result, are guided by the framework but are dependent on the diversity of participants having that conversation, and the manner in which it is facilitated. By the close of the conversation, groups are clear about their strengths and areas to improve and, most importantly, have some clear actions to improve the most important practices which will make the biggest difference to their performance.

We have used the self-assessment approach for a wide variety of topics including engineering operations, learning and development, analytical capability, business improvement and for the response to the human immunodeficiency virus, HIV/AIDS. Based on this experience, and the experience of many others, we can confirm that the process can be used for many other topics. In this chapter we'll show you how to go about it for yourself.

We will cover:

- Deciding who will use the framework, and who should be invited to create the first draft.

- How to go about selecting the practices.

- Understanding that each practice is likely to have more than one variable. The decision is how best to combine the variables to describe five levels.

- Defining the levels.

- Considering the benefits of global versus local frameworks.

- Self-assessment and strategy.

Deciding Who to Involve

Before starting out, there is a critical question which you should ask yourself: Who you are doing this for, i.e. who will be involved in using the self-assessment?

This will not only include those who need to improve, but also those where the good practices reside. The AIDS Competence framework, which we'll cover later, has been used by many rural African and Asian villages, cities around the world, non-governmental organisations (NGOs), United Nations (UN) organisations and multi-national businesses! It was important to bear all of these 'customers' in mind when creating the framework.

At what level of detail should the self-assessment be used? If in an organisation, is it at the level of the whole organisation, department level, country office level or team level? For a country, is it at national level, district level, city or neighbourhood level?

There are no 'right answers' to this. Discuss this with the group and see what is most fruitful; it's surprising how universal a well designed self-assessment can be. If you have different frameworks for different countries then you may not be able to share results and knowledge between those countries. Similarly, if different partner organisations build their own self-assessment frameworks, then they cannot compare their strengths directly.

The self-assessment framework will be used by a group to identify their strengths (which they can build on, and share with others) and their areas to improve. It is applicable to a team or group of persons with different assignments and specialisations who have a common task or goal. In that way, they gain a deeper understanding of the team's capabilities. For example, I have had meetings with 40 diverse representatives of cities such as Lyons in France, Curitiba in Brazil and Durban in South Africa discussing their response to AIDS. Their feedback was encouraging. By using the self-assessment approach it was the first time that as a city, they had agreed on the priorities to focus on. What's more it had taken only two hours and, despite diverse backgrounds, they were enthusiastically sharing their experiences with each other!

Bring the Right People Together – Experience and Diversity

The first step is to call a meeting of experienced and knowledgeable people in the field. Try to bring together as many types of stakeholder as possible and, where possible, those with different viewpoints. You'll probably find that self-nominated experts usually step forward at this stage, but what you really need is a diverse mix: people with a range of experience, people who are actively 'doing it', operational people who are able to switch between their own specific experiences and a more generic practice to be shared. Between 10 and 20 people is a good number for this kick-off meeting.

Their objective is to put together an initial draft which can then be shared with many others to amend, test and improve it. Usually when people claim to be active in a given field, their focus is necessarily on a part of it, and not the breadth of it. It is important to involve a diverse set of people in this meeting, so that the full breadth of practices can be identified. The people should be a representative mix of the main users of the approach since this will ensure buy-in and avoid the 'Not Invented Here' syndrome when it comes to using it.

We are using 'How to run effective meetings' as an illustrative example. This is not really a treatise on how to improve meetings, but an example of a topic for self-assessment that every reader can identify with. We all have meetings, and we can usually think of ways in which they could be more effective, yet somehow we often end up having the same kind of ineffective meetings! Whilst much of this example will feel like common sense, in our experience it is not necessarily common practice. We hope that you will get some benefit from using it as a catalyst for a conversation about improving meeting effectiveness, as well as learning about the process of creating a self-assessment framework. Two benefits for the price of one!

In the case of an 'Effective meetings' self-assessment framework, you would invite participation from a group of people who are likely to run meetings, those that are looking to improve on what currently happens in their meetings and perhaps people who are involved in a wide range of meeting types, internal and external. You might also think politically about any key groups to involve in order to secure buy-in to the final product. Cultural diversity could also be a factor – the practices which underpin an effective meeting in Milan may be different from one in Mumbai. If Mumbai represents a significant group of people who will use the self-assessment, who will speak for them in this meeting?

Having considered all of the above, you should be able to come up with a shortlist for the group who will work with you to create a first draft of the self-assessment framework.

Identifying and Selecting the Practices

Creating the common framework and using a common language is a key part of the overall approach. We can only begin to share knowledge once we have agreed upon the scope – what's included in the topic, where we choose to draw the boundaries and what we mean by specific terms. When a close knit team or group who are inwardly focused are performing well, they naturally generate their own language which enables them to develop ideas more quickly without having to explain all that has gone before. That language can be confusing to those outside of the group. Often the same words or phrases are used to mean different things, or different words to mean the same thing; synonym syndrome!

When we are only dealing with the written word, there is an increased risk of misunderstanding. I bet each of us can think of an e-mail exchange where this was particularly true! Since the output from this meeting will be exactly that – the written word – it is important to check, and double-check the intended and implied meanings of the words you use.

With a diverse group of people knowledgeable about the subject you can build a draft in a day or two, although it may be better to split it into a number of shorter meetings with thinking time between. Having generated the first draft with the group, it is then important to circulate it more widely for comment. This will not only improve the quality of the self-assessment, but will also generate buy-in and ownership. People will be much more willing to use, and to advocate, something that they have had a hand in designing.

When building a self-assessment for the response to AIDS, we met in Chiang Mai, Thailand for a meeting where a number of diverse stakeholders shared their experiences and models. Everyone had a focus on a few practices, and everyone had a slightly different perspective. Some people took a high level view while others focused on the practical detail.

For example: 'Do we look separately at the vulnerable groups, children, sex workers, drug users etc., and address the specific practices associated with them, or do we look at identify and address 'vulnerability' as a topic?'

Within a week, the draft was being used in seven Thai villages and the feedback enabled refinement and simplification. It was then used in Africa and the practices were re-shuffled into a different sequence. After three months, changes to the framework were frozen for a year. It wasn't perfect at that point, but we were finding that people were focusing too much on the words and too little on the conversation which would lead to action to respond to AIDS.

Naming the Practices – Using Active Verbs

People will often label a practice with a single word or phrase. Encourage people to be more explicit and then get them to rephrase it using an active verb. After all what is a 'practice' if it doesn't include an action?

Let me give you an example: 'Communication' can become 'Communicate with all stakeholders' or 'Listen to the concerns of those involved' or 'Publish the results'. One of my trainers described words like Communication as 'Nominalisations' – which he describes as 'things that don't generate outputs which you can put in a wheelbarrow!' That's a good way of looking at it. What is the output of this activity, and can you hold it in your hands, or at least touch it?

The output of communication is ... well, lots of things potentially. The output of 'Communicate with all stakeholders' is 'a set of informed stakeholders'. You could squeeze at least one or two stakeholders into that wheelbarrow, along with some 'published results'!

We started on the framework for Operations excellence in BP by focusing on reliability of equipment, and costs –

after sharing the initial draft widely, and hotly debating the definition of reliability, we included Health and Safety, planned closures, unplanned stoppages, managing spares, leadership and teamwork. All of these practices can have an impact on operational performance, so building that common framework is a crucial starting point for knowledge-sharing.

You can expect lots of debate in this meeting as the group decide where to place the boundary of the topic. It's good to have people engaging in debate – it proves that they're awake! Don't stifle disagreement but use it to seek clarity. There is no right answer other than the agreed answer.

For our 'Effective Meetings' example, assemble the group and get them to bring with them any materials which describe 'what is already known'. This can be a framed set of ground rules hung up in their team meeting room, a reference from the Internet, a report on lessons learned.

Ask them also to bring along in their heads an experience of a meeting that has gone particularly well. It's a good idea to ask them to explain what their role was in this meeting, as this will associate them with the success and make them feel good.

Encourage all members of the group to share experiences and what has already been written, and from them to tease out the key elements. List these practices in some sort of natural sequence as a sentence.

In our example we came up with:

1. Design the meeting.

2. Prepare and share relevant material.

3. Get the right people into the meeting.

4. Everyone plays an active role.

5. Use agreed meeting processes.

6. Summarise and share decisions and actions.

Having agreed the practices, we now need to consider the different levels of capability.

Deciding the Variables

With the same or a similar group, explore each practice in turn. What is included in this practice? Typically there will be more than one item which varies between a basic level of practice and a high level of practice. Identify these attributes or variables. Assign the variable to the practice which has the biggest impact on competence.

For example, the practice of 'Planning work' for Engineering Operations might have variables of frequency of meetings, technology to monitor progress of plan and resource management. The group creating that framework had to define how these combined together to describe each level of performance for 'Planning work' based on their experience.

For the example of 'Effective Meetings' the variables for 'Design the Meeting' include:

- Is this a meeting for ideas or for making decisions?

- Are the purpose and desired outcomes clear?

- Is the venue a standard meeting room, chosen to reflect the agenda or virtual?

- Facilitated or not?

The 'Use agreed meeting processes' practice has variables of:

- decisions versus ideas generation;

- recording actions and use of templates;

- follow-up required to ensure outcome.

Once you have done this for all practices, it's a good moment to take a break and clear your head. Having thought broadly about the topic, the group are about to shift their mode of thinking and dive into the details. Caffeine can be a helpful input at this point!

Defining the Levels

Starting with a single practice and using either a computer projector or a large wall (Figure 3.1) identify level one at the bottom and level five at the top. What is the

Figure 3.1 Defining the levels on the wall.

best practice you have seen to date? Use that as the basis of describing level five.

(In a subsequent year you could look outside your own organisation and benchmark with organisations – perhaps outside of your sector – which are recognised for that particular practice. However, for the first year we suggest that you look for the best examples internally. You know that it is possible to achieve this within your organisation – it's a quick win.)

What is the minimum basic acceptable level? Make that level one. Consider whether all the variables have been mentioned and whether a change will improve the competence of the organisation. There is no need to force all of the variables into all five levels. You might find one variable which is relevant for describing levels one to three, and another variable which is relevant for levels three to five only. This is perfectly natural, and usually makes for a less repetitive, more readable self-assessment.

Having staked out levels one and five, interpolate a level three – a good average level. Work through all practices at level one, three and five, ensuring that the levels are consistent in the way they describe each capability.

When refining the AIDS Competence assessment, the group used a key to describe each level:

Level Five   represents Lifestyle; this practice has become an unconscious competence, and this is the way we do things around here on a daily basis.

Level Four   represents Scale; we are applying the action broadly and sustainably.

Level Three   represents Action; we are responding to external prompts but are also being proactive.

Level Two   represents Reaction; we know the basic facts and are responding to external prompts.

Level One   represents Knowledge; we know the basic facts about this practice.

You may find that the above key to the levels also works for your self-assessment framework, or you may want to redefine particular levels. For example, level five might represent 'Continuously improving'. However you choose to describe the levels, it is helpful to the people developing the statements to have the key in mind.

Focus on Strengths and Use Positive Language

Try not to use negative language! Instead look for a way of expressing what you want to say positively. We have learned that we can achieve more by focusing on the positives. That is the essence of Appreciative Inquiry or Positive Deviance techniques.

Appreciative Inquiry involves asking questions to increase the value of what already exists. Appreciating strengths in others requires a shift in paradigm of how we work. Taking issue with the tendency to highlight deficiencies should not be interpreted as suggesting that all the news is good. Rather we have a choice about what we see in each other, in our working environments, in our families and our most intimate relationships – we even have a choice about what we see in ourselves.

If you observe any community in a stressful situation, you will find some members who are able to survive, or even prosper, when to the casual observer they have no more resources available to them than to their less successful peers. These are the positive deviants.

The Save the Children Fund in Vietnam was dealing with malnutrition. They observed that a small minority of poor families had children who were well nourished. It focused a 'positive deviant' (PD) approach on these resilient children. How do poor families have well nourished children when their neighbours with similar resource constraints do not? In other words, what is their 'deviant' behaviour? These households were feeding their children free or inexpensive tiny shrimps and crabs found in rice paddies plus sweet potato greens and were also feeding them more frequently during the day. Save the Children encouraged villagers to take responsibility for their own nutritional development.

Our early efforts in BP often focused on what was not being done in level one – 'deficiencies'. Unsurprisingly people were very reticent to assess themselves at that level!

Here is a comparison (Table 3.1) from two different self-assessment frameworks, HIV/AIDS Competence and HR Policy, to illustrate the point. The HIV/AIDS Competence example is a good illustration of using the key and positive language. The HR example from another organisation is rather more negative and people are unlikely to assess themselves at the lower levels. Read them from the bottom up, from level one to level five. How does each one make you feel as you read it?

Divide and Conquer

Depending on the number of practices identified, you may well want to divide into a number of small groups at tables (five or six people is ideal), and select a practice for each group to work on. This will create a little friendly competition, and keep things moving for you. It also ensures that the quieter members of the group have more opportunity to be heard.

However, we suggest that you first choose one practice to work on together in parallel, getting each table first

TABLE 3.1 Positive language.

Levels	HR Policy Reward & Recognition	HIV/AIDS Acknowledgement & Recognition
5	All staff feel their contributions are valued, recognised and rewarded.	We go for testing consciously. We recognise our own strength to deal with the challenges and anticipate a better future.
4	Most staff feel valued and appropriately recognised as individuals and teams	We acknowledge openly our concerns and challenges of HIV/AIDS. We seek others for mutual support and learning.
3	A reward and recognition system is in place but inconsistently applied.	We recognise that HIV/AIDS is affecting us a group/ community and we discuss it amongst ourselves. Some of us get tested.
2	People see little connection between performance and reward.	We recognise that HIV/AIDS is more than a health problem alone.
1	People feel victimised and blamed.	We know the basic facts about HIV/AIDS, how it spreads and its effects.

to work on the same practice and then share their description of the three levels. You'll probably find strong similarities in the description of the levels between the groups, but also some differences which will improve the final draft. Working on one practice in parallel in this way will give the members of the group confidence to trust each other enough to share out the remaining practices.

After the first exercise together, break the group into subgroups of five or six people and tackle the other practices in the same way, sharing them between the subgroups. Encourage people to trust their colleagues in the drafting phase – there will be time at the end to review and enhance each other's work. A useful ground rule for doing this is to discourage negative criticism and offer a replacement phrase or sentence to be considered by the original authors.

Having finished this, consider the overall framework in plenary session. Does this now describe the subject field completely – can you recognise the breadth of practices and the typical levels of competence exhibited somewhere in the organisation? Are there gaps or overlaps to be tackled?

Once this is completed to your satisfaction fill in levels two and four and wordsmith the resulting matrix of practices and levels. If you have run out of time in the meeting, or sense that the participants' energy is flagging, then ask for a subgroup who volunteer to take it away and complete it. Wordsmithing with a group of 20 is at best inefficient, and at worst destructive!

At this stage we suggest that you close the meeting and get the participants to try it out with some wider groups, perhaps their own teams or organisations, to test what issues it brings up. Using it on ourselves to start with is usually a good test of whether we have the right language to engage people in identifying their strengths and weaknesses.

Developing our 'Effective Meetings' Example

To illustrate this, let's look at our example, 'Effective Meetings', where we have a practice entitled 'Agree a common purpose and desired outcomes'. Let's look at how the content for levels one to five was derived.

The basic level is that we have an agenda, a location and a time for the meeting. Looking at the variables for this practice, the basic level (level one) would be agenda fixed by whoever calls the meeting, in the usual meeting room, called without warning. *Does that sound familiar to you?*

When we created our vision of an ideal meeting for level five, it included being well prepared, having a shared purpose, clarity about what we hope to deliver from the meeting, an agenda, with the time allotted for individual items and who will lead, and circulated two weeks beforehand. The location would be carefully selected depending on the nature of the meeting and what we want to achieve – potentially in the office, in a neutral venue or in a coffee shop.

To create level three, we selected variables in between level one and level five, ignoring some and choosing the middle of the scale in others. Describing levels two and four was then simply a matter of refining the differences, using the guiding phrases (the key for each level) of 'reacting to others' for level two and 'going to scale', that is 'all meetings' not 'some' for level four.

We ended up with a framework that looked like this (Figure 3.2):

Figure 3.2 Self-assessment framework for effective meetings.

Having completed the content for all the levels in the framework, we tested it with others. Had we missed critical practices, were there overlaps and gaps since there are some interactions between practices? We also spent some time checking our variables and making levels consistent across the practices.

We'll explain how to use it in the next chapter. If you can't wait and want to try it out now, to improve your next meeting or just to read the descriptions of each level of competence, you'll find it in Appendix A!

Meanwhile, let's look at some real examples in use:

Story 1 – Using Self-assessment to Unite a Consortium of Companies

onesixsigma.com was launched in 2003 as an online information resource for Six Sigma professionals, primarily in Europe. The objective was to create an effective medium for advertising jobs and services within a market sector that was spawned from GE's widely popularised management approach and growing rapidly across the Atlantic. In order to achieve this, the onesixsigma team developed an Internet portal containing white papers, interviews, newsletters and discussions, all sourced from real business case studies. This focal point was successful, drawing the attention of thousands of newly trained and certified practitioners, all seeking to share knowledge and tools for improving the business and innovating products and services – a virtual community was born. Management consultants, training and software providers flocked to advertise and promote this new way of doing, and improving business.

The forum filled up with questions, fuelled by challenges not just in learning tools or applying techniques but in managing change and influencing senior managers in this new way of conducting business. Many organisations in Europe shared the same issues and were drawn together in collaboration to solve the problems that faced them. Informal meetings were organised, where practitioners and leaders would meet to discuss common barriers to change that were impacting return on investment in this newly trained capability. A network of trusted relationships between approximately 20 organisations developed and through continuity, honesty and a self-organised code of conduct where attendance of consultants was restricted. This was a differentiator from commercial conferences, and a strong value proposition for the community. onesixsigma.com was becoming more than a virtual community – it was becoming a Community of Practice.

At the same time, the methodology itself was evolving and with it the scope of discussion and content. The meaning of Six Sigma varied from one organisation to another as it was blended with other techniques old and new. The most common criticisms were the time taken to implement it, the heavy investment in training tools and techniques that were not always applicable to every department and the use of alien terminology especially in non manufacturing environments. It became obvious that Six Sigma was not the answer to every problem but it was one of many enablers to the delivery of vision and strategy, to improving and innovating. Though the onesixsigma.com domain was created primarily for practitioners working with the Six Sigma methodology, the group and wider practice became more aware of other organisations with related challenges and different approaches to improvement. What about the organisations using LEAN or Kaizen? What about companies with a focus on innovation as well as excellence? This recognition that the 'brand' was in danger of being perceived as being methodologically exclusive led to the concept of the improvement and innovation (i&i) community.

The i&i Community of Practice was launched in the summer of 2008 with 10 founding members including Credit Suisse, Shell international, Sun Chemical, Royal Mail, Vodafone and TNT Express. At their inaugural meeting, the group experienced a presentation on BP's Operational Excellence approach which inspired them to consider how as a network they could improve the quality of their knowledge-sharing – relying less on serendipitous conversations and making more purposeful connections between members.

The first step was to create a common language – what did each organisation mean when they spoke about 'business improvement'? What did the term 'innovation' mean to the member companies? A small working group representing five of the member companies agreed to meet and create a self-assessment tool. One of the group, Vodafone, agreed to host the meeting at their headquarters.

> I was really inspired when I first saw the 'rivers approach'
> being presented – so I jumped at the chance to host the

first workshop to thrash out a common assessment tool with other founder members of the i&i community. It was all about getting a greater return on time invested in the network – and the potential prize was in our hands.

Irfan Ali – Business Improvement Specialist, Vodafone

Generating Buy-in by Building a Self-assessment Tool

The field of Business Improvement is no stranger to reference models and maturity matrices, and has a plethora of frameworks and definitions to bring to the table. It was recognised that with five different interested parties, each would have their own particular favourite model. So it was proposed that this group would work together to draw the best topics and content from all available materials – supplementing it where appropriate with their own experience and viewpoints on what 'good' looks like. Working in two small groups, the teams analysed the existing models and suggested 8–10 key capabilities for Business Improvement. The two groups then compared notes and combined their lists into a single set of ten key capabilities. These included:

- Leadership and Executive Ownership;

- Employee Engagement;

- Performance Focus;

- Consistency of Approach;

- Effective Deployment and Governance.

Having agreed on the capabilities, the two groups then re-formed to work on the content for the five levels. The prospect of filling 50 sheets of A4 with detailed content drawn from combined experience and established models daunted them. Rather than attempting to 'wordsmith' the details for all five levels, the participants agreed that they would produce the text for levels one, three and five. It was felt that the most valuable use of the experience in the room was to generate the draft content in bullet-point format. The missing levels could be added later by a smaller team, who would also har-monise the language and style across the different measures and levels.

An example taken from the Employee Engagement capability above – level five performance was defined as:

Employees feel proud of their contribution to improve-ment and feel empowered and committed to make change.

Employees feel listened to and are confident that their feedback will be acted on.

There is a clear policy which establishes Improvement activities as development opportunities.

Whilst the reference to and augmentation of existing models was contentious at times, the final product was well-debated – and members of the working group had a strong sense of ownership. One of the participants was heard to comment: 'It's not until you try to build one of these things that you really think hard about the content and how it all fits together.'

To reinforce the sense of co-creation – building something new together – a larger-than-life self-assessment tool was built up on one of the walls in the Vodafone office using a number of sheets of A4 paper (Figure 3.3).

Each one represented a cell in the self-assessment tool. As each group produced the sheets for levels one, three and five for a specific capability, they would come forward and proudly

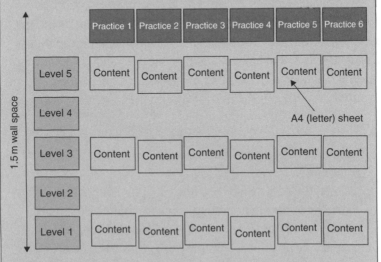

Figure 3.3 Creating the self-assessment on the wall.

stick their pages up on the wall before choosing the next capability to work on. This way of building up the big picture generated a sense of momentum, celebration of progress and some gentle competition between the two groups.

Having completed the large-scale self-assessment on Vodafone's bright red and grey walls, the group allowed themselves a moment's celebratory coffee, before testing out the self-assessment, based on their own organisation's scores. This walk-through generated further refinements, comments and questions which were captured on post-it notes on the wall. The raw output from the meeting was then refined by two members of the group, giving it a consistent style. Finally, it was circulated to the wider group of i&i members for one final round of constructive criticism before being finalised as the 'official version', owned and used by the network.

Since creating the Business Improvement Self-assessment, the team at i&i have encouraged the existing member companies to use the tool and share their scores and priorities for improvement with the other members of the network. As new organisations join the network, the self-assessment works as a powerful induction tool.

Sophie Smiles, i&i Director explains:

Potential new members of the i&i Community often ask us 'how do your existing members define the term "improvement"?' I can then talk them through the self-assessment to explain not only what we mean by 'improvement', but all the detail which underpins our model at each level. Members use the self-assessment to identify opportunities and connections to share good practice, and it provides the i&i team with a framework of reference to focus all activities and content on common issues – and therefore deliver outstanding value to our members.

Sophie concludes:

As far as the i&i Community is concerned, the best thing about the self-assessment is that it belongs to them. They helped to build it and they are free to use it as a health-check inside their organisation, as well as a framework for sharing knowledge with other i&i members. For i&i and our members, it's a source of competitive advantage which we all had a hand in creating and will continue to improve.

(Included with thanks to i&i: www.improvementandinnovation.com.)

The story which follows is an example from a network of Learning and Development (L&D) professionals working in government:

Story 2 – Helping UK Government Departments to Develop and Learn

Nestling in a corner of leafy Berkshire in England, the National School of Government (NSG) is a business school and government department in its own right, and is the leading provider of training and professional development to the public sector in the UK. According to its website, 'it aims to help public sector organisations build capacity in good governance and offer more effective, better value services, in partnership with other public service academies, professional institutes, business schools and universities'.

Graham O'Connell is Head of Organisational Learning & Standards and as part of his role, facilitates an informal network of around 60 learning and development professionals representing over 40 government departments and public sector organisations. The network meets quarterly, varying its format and focus depending on the needs of the members – sometimes an external speaker, sometimes a workshop or networking format – addressing a shared challenge.

He saw the creation of a common self-assessment tool (maturity matrix) as a golden opportunity to strengthen the network in several ways, stating:

> People in Government are good at sharing; they are quite generous because of the non-competitive nature of what they do. This whole approach is about giving a slightly more structured way to help people share when they come together. Also, there is another agenda – we all assume that we know 'what good looks like'. We read articles, talk to colleagues, go to conferences – but actually do we really know what good looks like and how we compare with it? This was a great opportunity to come together and crystallise – to piece together all

the little bits of the puzzle and to provide a holistic view of all those key things that make up L&D.

After all, if people in L&D can't be learning from each other, then who can? People are keen not to reinvent the wheel, and to collaborate at an intellectual or strategic level even if they can't collaborate directly on the delivery of training. People also want to know that they're not being left behind. At a personal level, those in smaller departments or at a senior level can be isolated and not have many people to bounce ideas off. Of course, there are plenty of conferences and events, but it is always great to come together with a close group of people in similar situations in other public sector organisations. I suspect half of the perceived benefit from the exercise probably came from that personal networking. But they needed a purposeful rationale to get together – that was the creation of our L&D Maturity Matrix.

The following message was sent to the network, inviting them to participate in a two-day workshop to build the maturity matrix.

Ever wanted to benchmark your L&D function against a model of good practice ... and get to network with others to find out what works for them and why?

You are invited to join us for a unique opportunity. We are inviting a cross section of representatives from L&D across Government to help co-create a Maturity Matrix for L&D – a sort of template for agreed good practice and mechanism for rating where you are against key criteria. This is an established technique in Knowledge Management and has been used by Chris Collison who will be our guest facilitator for the event.

The product of these two days will be a practical tool you can use back in your organisation, a broad assessment of the strengths and development areas for L&D in your organisation, and some peer contacts who may be able to help you raise your game in just the right places.

This Forum Event will cover:

• What is a Maturity Matrix and how it works

• Building a Matrix for L&D in Government

• Gauging where you are and your priority development areas

• Creating 'River' and 'Stairs' Diagrams

• Networking with peers and sharing the keys to good practice

The deal works like this: you get an interesting and useful two days, and all the benefits of working through a leading edge technique. We get your input to make sure the Maturity Matrix is a robust and meaningful tool. We all get to network and learn from each other.

Interested?

In response to this invitation, a small working group of eight L&D professionals (senior training managers or heads of L&D) met in the autumn of 2007 for a two-day workshop to create the self-assessment tool. During a facilitated session, working in two groups, they came up with seven core capabilities:

- Evaluating Success

- Business Alignment

- Supporting a Learning Culture

- Providing Development Options

- Managing the L&D Function

- Influencing Stakeholders

- Assuring Professional Delivery.

Looking at the choices of the group, Graham reflected on the L&D function:

There weren't any big surprises in the seven capabilities which the group identified. However, compared to five years earlier, there was much more focus on relationship management and influencing stakeholders, finding your way through organisational politics. There was less focus on the delivery of training courses. It was a richer, more strategic conversation.

On day two, the group worked on the detail of the levels of reach of these seven capabilities to create a maturity matrix with full details for each level. The full L&D self-assessment is provided in Appendix B, with thanks for its inclusion to the National School of Government.

Having completed the matrix and after an excellent National School lunch, the eight participants then put their newly created matrix to the test, giving scores for their own organisations, and identifying their priority areas for improvement. As in previous examples, these scores were converted immediately into a River Diagram and Stairs Diagrams, showing the potential for learning and sharing that existed within the room – just eight members of a network of over 60. Using the insights from the River and Stairs, the remainder of the day was spent delivering on the final promise in the invitation: 'Networking with peers and sharing the keys to good practice'. This took the form of a number of 'Peer Assists' on the topics where there was the widest range of capability, and the strongest desire to improve.

The finalised assessment was then shared with the wider network, and the workshop participants offered to assist other members with the benchmarking approach. Interestingly, though, Mark Cole, Head of Learning & Development at Queen Elizabeth Hospital NHS Trust and one of those involved in the exercise, realised that the model had wider application back in the workplace.

'My Trust had been concerned for some time as to how we might improve the patient experience,' he explained. 'There was considerable pressure on me, as an L&D person, to commission straightforward "customer care" training.' Mark felt that this very traditional response would not engage people in the process of improvement – and might not even have any short-term benefit. He argued that,

> Sheep-dipping people on such courses does not go to the root cause of poor customer service. I needed a response that involved staff and managers thinking about their practice and working together to find ways to improve it. I thought that the maturity matrix approach – getting staff to build a model of good quality user experience of our service – had a better chance of creating a culture change across the Trust.

He valued the approach for another reason as well:

> Our data showed that we needed to improve the way we communicated and worked with all our service-users – and one another. But the metrics gave a helicopter view of what happened across the Trust and so failed to acknowledge that there was good practice buried away in our day-to-day work. The model allows for the organisation to learn from itself and for staff to recognise where they do things well – and where they need to improve.

Mark was disappointed that events have somewhat overtaken him in regard to using this approach; his Trust is scheduled to merge with two others in South East London and so the patient experience work has slowed a little. Nevertheless, he remains enthusiastic about the model.

The challenge of pulling three organisations together – and getting their management and staff to agree on a new and unified approach to the way in which service is delivered – is enormous. And of course we need to ensure that our new Trust starts on the right foot in terms of managing the service-user experience effectively. In that sense, I see even greater opportunity to apply the model in an even wider range of organisational settings.

Where Does the Maturity Matrix Fit Today?

Two years later, the NSG has three main instruments to assure and measure L&D capability:

- The National School standards for L&D – these standards draw on elements from different L&D standards from around the world, contextualised for use in the UK public sector. Graham and his team use the standards for assurance and independent audit both inside the National School and with client organisations.

- An online *personal* self-assessment for L&D managers, helping them to assess the strategic positioning of their L&D function. This takes the form of a number of questions, for which an L&D manager would provide ratings and receive feedback and recommendations for improvement. This is a private assessment, the results of which are seen just by the L&D professional concerned.

- The Maturity Matrix described earlier, which came from the community and takes a broader view.

Graham continues:

> This last one is built around the idea of benchmarking, not just against the matrix, but using the matrix as a start point to connect up with other individuals across government. Together, these three tools are a set of concepts and resources which we can direct people to depending on what we notice about their needs. The maturity matrix is a start point – if I want to get from level 2 to level 4, I can sit in a dark room and try to figure it out, but wouldn't it be so much better if I talk with people who have already done that? It gives a light structure to what people do already – that is, to talk with others: 'You're doing this, you seem to be doing well – what can I learn from you?' We are using it as a medium to encourage people to learn from each other, in a less ad-hoc way than often happens through just networking.

He has also seen how the concepts in upper parts of the matrix have found their way into other NSG products:

> A lot of the higher level four and five items have informed the things we teach on our programmes for Heads of L&D and Training Managers. If they want to know what good looks like, we reference our matrix. We say 'A group of senior, experienced peers got together, and this is what they identified as good practice'. It gives it more credibility because it's rooted in real-life government L&D experience, rather than something out of a book!

Best Practice or Best Fit?

Graham has clear views about the ongoing development of the maturity matrix and its power to capture a snapshot of 'what good looks like' for a particular moment in time. He also has strong views about the often-cited concept of 'best practice'.

> We have done this exercise once with a particular group on a particular occasion, but it's a process that you can use on an ongoing basis to constantly refresh the content. New people come into the community – they need to feel ownership too. It's also a way of capturing your 'inheritance' – the learning that has gone before. Today, there might be different challenges, so we need to refresh it.

> I'm not a great believer in the concept of 'best practice' – that there is something out there at the top end that you can just copy. To me, it's more about 'best fit'. Best practice is a myth. Best fit is about working out what good looks like in your context. The matrix helped us to figure out exactly that for organisations in the central government arena.

Evolving the Matrix – Rivers Flood their Banks!

The NSG L&D network is a public sector group but the members are also part of other networks including private sector companies, which can introduce new thinking and new aspirations for 'what good could look like'. As Graham puts it:

> Over time, rivers erode or flood the banks, so there is a space where a level six needs to exist. We need to continuously evolve the matrix, based on practices within Government and trends in industry. However, we must be careful not to over-extend the boundaries, and put improvement unrealistically out of reach. Look at it this way – I speak schoolboy French and I can make sense of most conversations when I'm in France. If I go to China, I'm completely lost! Whilst there are benefits in exploring L&D practices from diverse sources, I can make the link much more effectively with organisations who are to some degree similar, where I can speak the same language. But there's a tension between the value of diversity, with its newness and difference, and 'closeness', where we understand the context and can more easily translate the learning to our own situation. It is all about balance.

Graham expects to see the Maturity Matrix continue to be referenced, applied and updated by the L&D Network, enabling them to continue to 'raise their game in just the right places'. The National School's L&D Maturity Matrix is available on its Virtual School L&D Community website.

(Included with thanks to the National School of Government: www.nationalschool.gov.uk)

The Benefits of Global Rather than Local Frameworks

One of the first things that organisations do when they see the potential of this approach is to tailor their own framework for *their own reality*. They believe that they are *different* and hence must design their own framework. Whilst this is completely understandable, our experience is that processes (or elements of them) are often transferable – more transferrable than people initially believe. If people can live with a more generic framework then the opportunity for sharing is much broader. The sharing can only take place as far as the same framework and language is shared, hence we would encourage using a global framework for discussion.

Depending on the participants, the conversation will of course be different, and the actions derived from it will rightly be local, appropriate to the participants and their sphere of influence. A UK Government Office we worked with used a self-assessment describing 'knowledge management' at two levels: general staff and director level. The scores were remarkably similar across all five practices, but the conversations around 'What can we do to close the gap', and resulting actions were very different.

If people locally really do feel they have some irreconcilable local differences, then our suggestion is to compromise and use a central core of practices so people can share widely, but allow say two or three additional practices which are relevant locally. By the time people have assessed against the global practices section, they usually find they can have all the conversations they need without adding the others.

Defining the Strategy

A director I knew once defined strategy as 'The few things to think about when deciding whether to invest resources or not'.

One thing which we have learned almost by accident is that the framework usually defines elements of that overall strategy. Whether the topic is 'Knowledge management' or 'Responding to AIDS', reading across level five in all practices will probably define your vision, the outcome of your strategy. Often, the levels leading up to level five will describe the journey we need to make.

Here is an example of level five from our five practices for Knowledge Management. Each is the level five description for the practice.

KM Strategy	Clearly identified intellectual assets. KM strategy is embedded in the business strategy. Framework and tools enable learning before, during and after.
Leadership	Leaders recognise the link between KM and performance.
Behaviours	The right attitudes exist to share and use others' know-how. Leaders reinforce the right behaviour and act as role models.

Networking	Networks and Communities of Practice have a clear purpose, some have clear deliverables, others develop capability in the organisation. Clearly defined roles and responsibilities. Networks meet annually.
Learning before, during and after	Prompts for learning built into business processes. People routinely find out who knows and talk with them. Common language, templates and guidelines lead to effective sharing.
Capturing knowledge	Knowledge is easy to get to, easy to retrieve. Relevant knowledge is pushed to you. It is constantly refreshed and distilled. Networks act as guardians of the knowledge.

Does that describe your vision of an organisation with effective knowledge management?

So the framework helps define the strategy (the few things you need to think about in order to decide whether to invest resources) – and each group gets to select its priorities for implementation.

Having looked in detail at the process for creating a self-assessment framework, let's now look at the process of using that framework with groups, to help them learn, share and improve. There's no time to sit back and admire your handiwork, the value will come from using the self-assessment to identify your strengths and who you can share with.

Applying the Approach

4

Having created your self-assessment framework, how do you go about making use of it? It's a tool to encourage a conversation - a dialogue, not a box-ticking exercise. Don't try filling it in on your own; talking to yourself doesn't count!

This chapter explores how to get the most from the self-assessment:

- The approach is all about sharing experience within a framework, creating the right environment for a useful conversation. It shows how you can identify your strengths and the focus for improvement, and how to explore the options for developing your capabilities.

- The self-assessment is subjective and it allows sensitive issues to be discussed without the emotion associated with 'audit'.

- It focuses you to build on existing strengths, on improving, and encourages you to own the issue and the response.

- Finally it challenges your assumptions, assumptions that you may not have been aware that you were making.

If you change your attitude to appreciate strengths rather than looking for and solving problems then you are more likely to recognise the competencies within your organisation.

It's All About the Conversations

To sit at your desk or computer and go through the self-assessment framework as an individual would be a mistake. It is important to talk about it, to realise that people have different perceptions, to share your own perceptions and hear what others' experiences have been. It's not about *what you would have liked to have happened* but rather *how you perceive things really are*. It is also vital that you are not so wrapped up in your own experience that you don't listen to others. You have to be motivated and ready to learn from others' experience.

Typically a group of people will sit down to discuss their perceptions of the levels of their team, department or group, based on the practices and levels of the self-assessment. Perhaps a group of 12 people talks together with a facilitator who ensures that each has their voice heard. Hierarchy should not influence the outcome; instead, it should be the balance of experiences which does. A larger group, 40 or more people, would typically be split into subgroups of six to 10 people at smaller tables so that everyone's voice is heard. Scores are shared, and then debate opens up till a consensus is reached. People are encouraged to give an example to illustrate what happens in their organisation at the level they propose.

'What do they experience happening?'
'What is missing that prevents the group being at a higher level?'

As different perceptions and experiences are aired, people see opportunities to improve, and gain insights as to how they might do that. Sometimes they decide to revise their scores in the light of examples from others.

Throughout the conversation, we are seeking consensus rather than compromise or simple score averages. Sometimes not all agree on the number but everyone will know what can be done to improve the situation in their area.

People challenge whether this process is objective. They are correct, it is not. 'But the words are too vague,' they say, 'People can interpret them the way they want to.' This is true. What is important is that those best placed to improve the practice have a conversation together to determine their relative strengths and areas for improvement and together decide what to change in order to improve. *It is the conversation that is important rather than the absolute level.* This is not a beauty contest!

There is no prize for having the highest score. The reward is the opportunity to learn from, and share with, others to improve the overall performance of your organisation.

It is important to get the right people representing the group into the conversation. All stakeholders should be represented with a 'diagonal slice', that is a range of people representing different departments or sections of the community, or different geographical areas, and different levels of the hierarchy to get a wide range of experiences and to ensure ownership of the response everywhere.

When they start the discussion, you'll frequently hear people disagreeing. That's healthy, so don't attempt to stifle it. The facilitator needs to ensure that the participants focus on the issue rather than the person. When they have discussed the issue from various perspectives, they decide to move forward on the basis of what was said. Their response should be absolutely practical and concrete because the action is centred on their own context.

Involving the Procrastinators

'Procrastination is the thief of time', according to Edward Young, the eighteenth century English poet. In the context of self-assessment, it can be the 'thief of action' too. There may be times when you encounter people who are less receptive to a self-assessment, particularly if they took no part in constructing it. One of the practical barriers which we have encountered is that some people prefer to spend their time discussing the appropriateness of the practices and the content of the levels within them, rather than discussing how they assess themselves against the practices. Whether they are procrastinating, feel uncomfortable with the idea of assessing themselves, or whether they think their circumstances are different and unique, is a matter of conjecture. Whatever the case, you need to find a way to un-hook them from debating the content and engage them with the activity of self-assessment, sharing and learning.

Sharing the Dream

We have used a technique that helps people to accept the content of a self-assessment matrix and start applying it. The approach involves 'sharing your dreams'; here's how you apply it.

With the group all together, introduce a 'dream session' or 'vision session', which allows people free reign to develop a common vision of what Utopia might look like, and helps them to see how a combination of their personal visions can map against the self-assessment.

The steps are as follows:

- Individually, draw your dream on a sheet of paper.

- In small groups, share your personal dreams with each other.

- Create a collective 'shared dream' for each small group.

- Share the collective dreams from all groups whilst capturing key phrases.

- Show how the key phrases are incorporated into the practices and content of the self-assessment, discussing any exceptions and agreeing actions.

The example below is used by the Constellation for AIDS Competence (www.aidscompetence.org). Firstly, each individual spent a few minutes considering what an AIDS Competent community might be like – however they cared to imagine it. They then each used a blank sheet of A4 paper and felt pens to draw something to represent such a community. Some people interpreted this literally and drew pictures incorporating medical centres, village halls and schools. Others took it more figuratively and drew pictures with hearts or small groups of people supporting one another. Whatever they choose was correct, because it was their dream and they were entitled to share it in this way.

It's worth noting that this is not meant to be treated as an exercise in showing off artistic prowess! Rather, it is a prompt for people first to think about and then to talk about their vision. Some prefer to share their dream verbally. Drawing a picture rather than writing a description encourages people to exercise the creative side of their brain. The picture of a dream drawn by a group in Cambodia is a good example of this (Figure 4.1).

Figure 4.1 Cambodia – community dream.

Having illustrated their personal dreams, the participants then formed into groups of five or six people to share their dreams with each other. They took time to explain it to the others, and the group asked questions about each other's dreams, clarifying anything which was unclear. The intent was twofold: to understand (rather than judge) each other's dreams and to encourage further dreaming. Five groups did the same exercise in parallel. Once they had completed this in their small groups, they were asked to draw another dream on a flip chart. This had to be a single 'dream' which embraced the other five dreams.

Meeting this challenge is more than a simple matter of pasting the six pictures on to one sheet. Rather, the six need to work together to create a shared dream which embraces the ideas of each of their dreams, and ultimately is broader than any single dream.

Once this was completed, they shared their dream with the other groups. This created a sense of alignment in the room; a common sense of the direction in which they were all moving. Whilst working through this process, people came to recognise similarities in the dreams as well as things they had not thought of.

As they were sharing their dreams, a facilitator captured in the background the key words and phrases illustrated by the dreams and linked them directly with the practices of AIDS Competence. Once everyone had finished sharing, the facilitator explained what she had been doing. The facilitator related the words used to describe the dream or vision – the actual words or phrases that people have used – to the self-assessment matrix and particularly to the headings of the practices.

Normally there is a good overlap, but occasionally there are practices on the self-assessment matrix which have been missed from the dreams. This leads to a discussion as to whether it would improve the dream if it were added. This is usually the case. Less frequently, there might be a practice suggested by the dreams which is missing from the self-assessment matrix. The participants can then discuss whether this practice needs to be added, or if it can be discussed within the content under the heading of one of the other practices.

This process is important because it ensures real alignment in the room of the shared vision of success – of the destination people have in mind. People can then decide upon the actions they need to take to move towards it. The route they take to the destination may be similar or different, and they may travel together or at a different pace. Ultimately, the 'sharing your dream' technique gains real ownership of the self-assessment matrix so that the conversations focus on sharing strengths and experience and how to improve the level of competence which, of course, is exactly where that focus should be.

The Environment

We cannot stress too highly the importance of participants having the right attitude at the outset. Put simply, the self-assessment approach is used to identify what knowledge to share and with whom. But we must be looking for strengths rather than problems and we must recognise the ownership the approach engenders through meaningful conversation. When we talk glibly about 'managing knowledge', we are really talking about *creating the environment for knowledge to flow* from those who have it to those who need it, when and where they need it. A mix of attitudes, processes and technology can help to support the right environment for that to happen. So how can we create that environment?

Setting the Right Tone

The approach relies on setting the right tone at the earliest stages of the meeting. That means starting by looking for strengths in others before pressing our own solutions. From our own experience, when we facilitate a self-assessment session, we start by explaining the process of the meeting. We acknowledge that, although the participants are sharing the way they do it, and what they experience when they do it that way, they are not advocating that others must do it the same way as them. We cannot declare that the way we do it is 'best practice', or even 'good practice' if we have not tried other ways. Unfortunately the balance of advocacy and inquiry isn't always the right one, and participants can leave a meeting feeling that they have had a 'best practice' forced upon them.

Tuning Our Listening

Tuning our listening is important. There are some clear distinctions in how we listen. When we are speaking, we all have mechanisms to give us time to think what to say next – speech fillers such as 'um', 'err' or 'you know', a draw on a cigarette, a cough, a swallow or a sip of water. Sometimes we let someone else speak while we think what to say next without really listening to what the other person is saying. ('Never!' we hear you exclaim! Think about those meetings where we go round the table in order, making our introductions. Are we really listening to who is in the room or are we thinking of what to say about ourselves that will impress?)

As you read these paragraphs what are you thinking right now ...? Are you listening to evaluate, 'Is that right? Is that wrong?' Or 'What can I ask to make myself look good/not look bad?' Perhaps you are thinking, 'How can I use this when I next talk to my partner?' Or listening for how it fits with what you already know?

Practice listening to understand; suspending judgement until you have had the chance to really comprehend what someone is telling you in their own context. Only then can you evaluate it and decide what you are going to do with what you have learned.

A tip: A simple mechanism for changing the attitude to listening and sharing across your organisation is to get managers who visit a number of offices to habitually ask 'Who did you learn from in doing this task?' And 'Who else would benefit from knowing what you have just learned?'

Probably the biggest impact you can make is to change your own attitude. However humble and modest we might be, we have an egocentric view of the world. If we can shift our attention to focus on connecting local exchanges of knowledge rather than being the hub to which all knowledge is offered then more connections are made and hence there are more conduits for knowledge to flow. Too often Headquarters staff, or a 'Centre of Expertise', is the focus and possibly the bottleneck for sharing knowledge. They are often the ones who decide best practice; and they are the ones who learn most from the collected lessons. However, some of the most relevant knowledge is local, the practice is best applied locally, and a better role for headquarters staff is to facilitate local-to-local exchange of knowledge.

Social networking has a key role in establishing an environment where knowledge gets to the parts of the organisation where it is most needed. Say to yourself 'I bet someone out there has already done what I am about to do. I wonder who and what community of people I should ask?' In today's highly connected, fast-moving world the challenge is knowing where to place your request, as there are many different forums and technologies available. Start close to home with the people and communities that you know, and trust in the connections they can make for you.

Identifying Strengths

So how do we create the right environment for a self-assessment session? Firstly, encourage those in the discussion to focus on appreciating people's strengths. Ask the group to explore collectively what more they can do to build on these strengths. Identify areas of weakness and consider who is already doing it better and then how best to help transfer the knowledge without getting in the way.

We must remember that we have a choice. We can look at 'what works' or we can look for 'what doesn't work' – whatever we look for is what we are likely to find!

All too often we choose to problem-solve (rather than looking for a strength to build on and repeat), and often we choose to solve someone else's problem. This approach shifts the paradigm, from making an intervention in order to solve someone else's problem (and in the process making them 'the victim'), to facilitating a group to identify their own strengths and supporting them to build on these to come up with their own solutions.

Let's look at some real examples of applying the approach.

Story 3 – Responding to AIDS in Brazil

We were in a large meeting room without windows in the basement of a municipal building in the centre of Curitiba, a forward-looking city in Southern Brazil. An assortment of 40 people were gathered there at a series of round tables. The usual bottles of water, name-cards, notebooks and pens adorned the tables.

They were all assembled to discuss the city's response to AIDS, in preparation for meeting with 14 other Brazilian cities to share how they respond to the issues of HIV/AIDS at a city level. People represented the health department, the mayor, charities, civil society groups — including people living with AIDS — and businesses. There was an air of inquisitiveness and expectation; they had not been through a self-assessment before, and although they had seen the paperwork, they didn't quite know what to expect. There was a sense of nervousness.

They discussed each practice in turn, in small groups. People were animated and passionate, determined to make their point. The participants were listening well, pleased to have the chance to share their experiences and truly interested in each other's experience. It was clearly something they didn't do often, if at all. Laughter broke out in some groups. When they shared their scores and found differences between groups they were quick to justify their choice of level with an illustrative example. The first practice took nearly 30 minutes to explore, as everyone wanted to be heard, regardless of the appropriateness of their example! However, as they became accustomed to the process, they sped up and contributed only relevant examples. From the different perceptions and experiences, they began to build a picture of what their shared response could be.

In time they got to the last of 10 practices which was entitled 'Mobilising resources'. They discussed the topic in their groups, and then shared their capability levels with the room. With one eye on the clock, the representative of the Health Department tried to cut the discussion short – 'Well clearly we are at level four on this practice. We have adequate funds for HIV/AIDS and ensure treatment is provided to all those who require it. After all it is a legal requirement in Brazil.' A transgender person named Lisa, leapt up from the table to disagree. Lisa was representing a minority civil society group with a real interest in the city's response to AIDS. She proceeded to give a powerful example of why the city was only at level one currently. The Health Department representative listened thoughtfully and they had a conversation as though they were the only ones in the room; everybody else was silent, listening intently. They truly tried to understand each other's perspective – there was no personal antagonism. They realised what they could each do to make the response better than it currently was, and each committed to actions to move it forward. The air was cordial and all left feeling content that they had had their say, that they all had a realistic picture of the current state and also had some actions for improving the response. They were in good shape to share their strengths and know what they wanted to learn from the other Brazilian cities at a meeting they were hosting the following week.

Sharing Experience Within a Framework

Regardless of the topic, the self-assessment framework provides a common frame or set of practices and a common language to enable people to share across the breadth of the topic. By systematically discussing each practice, the group can cover the whole topic rather than 'talk past each other' or focus on the limited set of issues which they think are the most important. Often people feel they have an issue covered and they should be the ones to resolve it, when in fact it emerges they are dealing with only part of the problem or topic.

Here's a practical example. You are struggling with formatting a document in Microsoft Word on your computer and you mention your problem to a few people.

The IT guy recommends a cool new laptop with the Vista operating system.

Someone on the Helpline offers you a template you can always use and tells you where to download it from.

An acquaintance that you are talking to at the gym, who works for a different organisation, recommends a simpler word processor.

The Learning & Development co-ordinator recommends a two-day training course that's running next month.

Your teenage children have no idea how you could be having a problem with something as simple as Microsoft Word in the first place!

Each is seeing the solution to the issue from their own perspective. If they were brought together, these people (and others) could agree an overall framework which will deal with the topic holistically.

That deals with the breadth of the framework, but what about the common language?

People use the same words to mean different things or different words to mean the same things. I can still remember an interesting conversation at a school governors' meeting which I participated in. I talked about introducing some comments from parents anonymously, by compiling a list entitled 'Heard on the Street'. A fellow governor interpreted 'heard' as 'herd' and took exception to what I was saying thinking parents would not appreciate being likened to dumb animals, following one another aimlessly! It took several fruitless attempts to explain myself and eventually the intervention of the Chair. We clearly had different mental images of what we were talking about!

It is Subjective, and De-personalises the Emotion

The self-assessment framework allows people to talk about sensitive subjects without letting personal emotions get in the way. People focus on the framework and the levels, they discuss the phrases and how their experience illustrates it. They listen to understand the others' experiences, but their emotions are not focused on one other. People have different perceptions of what the capability at a specific level means, and by drawing on their personal experience – getting inside themselves and re-experiencing the feelings they felt before – they can compare and recalibrate levels. There is passion and creative tension, but the emotion is not directed destructively at a particular individual. The facilitator makes sure this is so.

The association between levels and practices helps people to think in a different way. They begin to express their ideas and feelings in different ways and the process is boosted, amplified, because there are others who can listen to, reflect and build on what they say. If you choose participants correctly, different people reflecting different perspectives, it enhances the honesty and openness in the room.

What amazed me was that ... people were talking in a different way from before. They were expressing some doubts. In a one-to-one discussion, yes, but in a meeting they don't normally say these things.

Luc Barrière Constantin of UNAIDS

It focuses people on improving and encourages them to own the response.

Self-assessment helps to put the issue under discussion in the broader context of all that needs to be done on the topic. This is a method which brings everybody together to assess what the priorities are. It also helps people to define a baseline, to set their priorities and then to take ownership of the response. When a group conducts a self-assessment, they first define their current position. Usually, they will have a feel for that in broad terms, but self-assessment forces them to consider exactly where they are positioned across the various practices. In the previous example on formatting a document, a number of people considered the issue from the user's perspective – the hardware, the brand and version of software, the templates and the training. The solution for that user was a combination of several of the alternatives, and together they evolved a process to get all users capable of formatting their own documents.

Once a group has worked through all the practices of the framework and has reviewed the current strengths and areas to improve for all of the practices, they can then decide what their priorities are and the level that they would like to get to in those priority areas after, say, 12 months or two years. Since it is self-assessment, they set their own priorities and so take ownership of those actions.

It Challenges Our Assumptions

Frequently the differences in perception about levels of capability unearth some hidden assumptions. Having exposed the assumptions we are making, we can consciously debate whether they really apply in our current setting. This often causes groups to reframe and reprioritise their response and can create breakthroughs. I can remember a 'Peer Assist' meeting where various businesses involved in the aviation industry came together to look at an industry-wide response to environmental concerns. At first, different businesses looked to preserve their own interests, but after a while, they started to look at the issue differently and came up with a scenario where the public had a notional 'ration' of environmental points to use and could choose to spend them on heating, driving to work or more overseas flights. Then it was in everyone's interest to make their offerings compelling to the public, and the priorities of the group shifted.

The Focus for Improvement

We're now at a stage where the group has had a lively discussion about what level they are at for each of the practices they are considering. Let's say that there are 10 practices in this particular example. Typically the group would have half a day for the conversation, ensuring that plenty of time was allocated so that issues get aired. The participants have identified their strengths (those practices for which they rate themselves at levels four and five) and their low-scoring practices. Now it is time for the group to decide what they want to improve.

Some of the participants are 'gung-ho' and ambitious, and want to reach level five for all 10 practices, but this is just not likely to be practical. By identifying no more than three practices to improve – the three which will have the greatest chance of making a difference – the group is forced to discuss what resources they have, what is achievable and what will have the greatest impact in their situation. The very act of prioritising and choosing makes another important contribution to the level of ownership and commitment to implementing the actions. Prioritising three practices to improve sets an agenda for the group doing the assessment for the next time period – 12 months perhaps. In the event that the group completes its actions and closes the gap in less than 12 months then they can reconvene, celebrate and reassess to determine the next three priorities. The difference between the current level and the target level defines the gap in performance.

Finding Ways to Close the Gap in Performance

Where can we look to close that gap? The first place to look for improvement ideas comes from the conversations the group have just had. Where there is a difference in perception of what level the group is currently at, it's worth probing further to see if there are some early 'outliers' of good performance. Perhaps one department is better at one practice. There are not enough instances to justify the higher score for the whole organisation, but certainly enough 'glimmers of light' to learn from.

The second place to look is at the River Diagram to determine whether other groups who have completed the self-assessment have already assessed themselves at a higher level. If there is river above your group's score, then this means that at least one other group has ranked itself more highly. Looking at the Stairs Diagram for that practice will tell you who. We'll explore this in more detail in the next chapter, but before we do let's take a look at three different examples: one from an international enterprise software giant looking to share knowledge across its professional communities, one from regional government in the UK looking to share knowledge between departments and then with partners, and finally an example from Nationwide (a mutual bank) wanting to improve knowledge-sharing along its supply chain.

Story 4 – Developing Professional Communities in Oracle

Communities of Practice are people-networks used by a large number of organisations as mechanisms for learning, sharing know-how, spreading good practice and improving performance. Perhaps the most widely held definition is provided by Etienne Wenger in his book *Cultivating Communities of Practice*, which offers that 'Communities of practice are groups of people who share a concern or a passion for something they do and learn how to do it better as they interact regularly.'

Oracle Corporation, the global software and services giant, relies heavily on communities of practice and virtual teams in the day-to-day running of its business. Communities in Oracle were first born in their Europe, Middle East and Africa region consulting business, in 2000. They were located in the sales organisation and given the title 'circles of excellence'. Since that time, these relatively informal groups have developed, taking on a more precise structure and deliberate governance, involving sponsorship from members of the executive team. Today, 'professional communities' (PCs), as they have come to be known, are seen as recognized tools to bridge the gaps of the often-changing formal organisational structure. Increasingly, they are evolving into more fluid groups of professionals making active use of Web 2.0 technologies to work together and draw in knowledge and skills whenever needed. A typical professional community draws its membership from more than 30 countries and will focus on an industry sector, for example Communications, combining their product and process knowledge to support a 'go-to-market strategy'.

Oracle's Professional Community Learning Event

In April 2006, professional community leaders participated in an intensive two-day learning event close to their European headquarters, focusing on virtual working and leadership. This continued a pattern of PC leader events, which had been held annually for several years; however, this event had a different style and focus from previous events, and involved the use of a self-assessment tool, a River Diagram, raft-building and a lake!

One of the aims of the event was to generate a common understanding of 'what good looks like' for an ideal community, and to encourage PC leaders to develop action plans to help them move towards this slate together. To achieve this, Oracle developed a self-assessment framework to benchmark the performance of its professional communities, and then to maximise the time that community leaders spent together as an opportunity for learning and sharing.

The framework described a range of capabilities from level one (basic performance) to level five (world-class) for five practices. These practices were agreed to be the core capabilities for successful community working in Oracle:

- Communication

- Developing Trust

- Virtual Leadership

- Cultural Understanding

- Sharing Good Practice.

The self-assessment set out in some detail what the various levels of performance should look like.

For example – to assess itself at level four (strong, but with scope to improve) for the practice of 'Communication', a professional community leader should be able to provide evidence of the following:

> Clearly defined communications plan using appropriate tools.
>
> Roles in virtual meetings are clearly defined to ensure participation and to capture actions.
>
> Glossary created to establish a common language and avoid jargon.
>
> Training provided on tools to ensure familiarity and comfort with technology.
>
> Website or shared drive has regular use and members contribute.

The leaders of each professional community first assessed their own performance individually, then invited input and supporting examples from other members of their PC. These scores were then shared with their peers, the other community leaders, at the face-to-face learning event. The common language of the self-assessment allowed the PC leaders to discuss their similarities and differences and to learn from each other's strengths. Having shared their stories and examples with their peers, the final task for each community leader was to choose two areas for improvement – the greatest priorities with the greatest return. Should we invest our effort in building trust and communication, or in techniques for sharing good practice? Which will lead to a better performing community? What is the best use of our limited resources?

The scores for each community were displayed as a River Diagram illustrating the range of scores for each measured capability. 'Who is at level five?' or in other words 'Who can I learn from?'; 'Where is the river widest?' and so 'Where is the greatest potential to learn from each other?'

The River Diagram highlighted the degree to which the community leaders had chosen to improve particular practices, and was used to create a supply and demand for sharing during the remainder of their time together and beyond the event. Having completed the self-assessment process and identified the opportunities for learning and sharing among themselves, the community leaders then spent the following day exploring each of the practices in detail as part of an in-depth learning session on virtual working. As part of this, each PC leader received their own copy of a book of hints, tips, guidance and good practices designed to further develop their capability. This book (*A Guide to Virtual Working*) was developed by Oracle in partnership with Willow Transformations in order to provide the participants with something physical to take away from the event and remind them of the key learning points.

Tales from the River, and the Riverbank!

The sources of learning were to come from two distinct sources:

1. Learning from the experience of other PC leaders. These learning opportunities could be clearly derived from the River Diagram, as it was easy to discover which PC leaders were scoring their communities at each level – and hence where the supply of learning could come from.

2. Learning from external input on good practices, captured in a specially designed 'virtual working handbook', designed to extend the capability of all of the PCs.

This handbook provided guidance on how to achieve levels four and the 'world-class' level five on the self-assessment – levels which no PC had managed to reach independently (see Figure 4.2). The learning had to come from beyond the river, on the 'north bank'

Taken together, these two learning inputs and the discussions which followed enabled the PC leaders to reflect, prioritise and

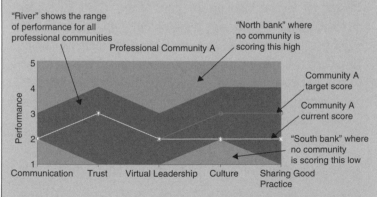

Figure 4.2 Oracle's Professional Community capability River Diagram. (Used with permission of Oracle Corporation UK Ltd)

develop improvement plans together. However, expecting the perfect 'knowledge-sharing marketplace' to appear instantly within a large group of PC leaders from several countries was a little ambitious, so Karen Eden (senior knowledge development manager, EMEA Applications & Industries) who organised the event, added one extra activity in the form of a physical challenge.

Building Trust – with a Splash!

Karen takes up the story:

> In our self-assessment, we had placed importance on the practices of communication, building trust, virtual leadership, understanding international culture and sharing good practices. With over fifty international managers travelling in for this event, we felt it was vital that we 'walked the talk' in the way we designed the two days. We wanted this group of PC leaders to act as a community in their own right, so the same capabilities applied to them as a group.

> We designed the event to ensure that the PC leaders had time and space to get to know and rely on each other, to experience the art of communication and leadership in culturally diverse groups – and perhaps most of all, to have fun together and create a memorable experience. The hotel where we met was on the edge of a lake, so we designed a raft-building competition at

the end of the first day, before the usual evening dinner and drinks together.

We assembled the PC leaders into eight teams and equipped them with rope, wooden planks and four empty oil drums. Their challenge was to design and build a raft in one hour, ready for a race against the other teams. It was a pity that it wasn't a river, or we could have made an even better connection with the river diagram which they had created together earlier!

Inevitably the day ended with nearly everyone getting wet, and later in the bar, plenty of discussion (not to mention a little light-hearted incrimination!) and reflection.

Getting into Action

The following morning, the PC leaders had developed noticeably deeper relationships with each other, and after a humorous look-back at digital photos of the previous day's lake-side activities, they set about the tasks of sharing their scores and action-planning.

Each PC leader recorded their scores personally, before discussing these with their peers. These discussions surfaced a number of examples and some constructive peer-challenge, after which each leader had the opportunity to revise their scores and targets.

Karen adds:

> It was interesting to observe how these peer-to-peer discussions were both challenging and supportive at the same time. The words in the self-assessment gave a structure to the conversations whilst the interaction between PC leaders provided the stories and evidence to support their scores and targets.

To guide this part of the day, groups of PC leaders were provided with A3-sized 'workmaps' to annotate. Each workmap included the self-assessment tool, a table for action planning (Figure 4.3) complete with dates, target and accountabilities. The workmap template also included space to record INSPIRATIONS & INNOVATION which arose as the PC leaders shared their experience and aspirations with their peers in small groups.

This part of the learning event was particularly successful, and in summing up her lessons from the event, Karen noted: 'Our community leaders learned more from their peers through self-assessment and peer-assists sessions than they did through direct training.'

Each PC leader left the event with:

- their copy of the *Guide to Virtual Working* and supporting training notes;

- a completed community planning workmap template with clear targets and priorities for the year;

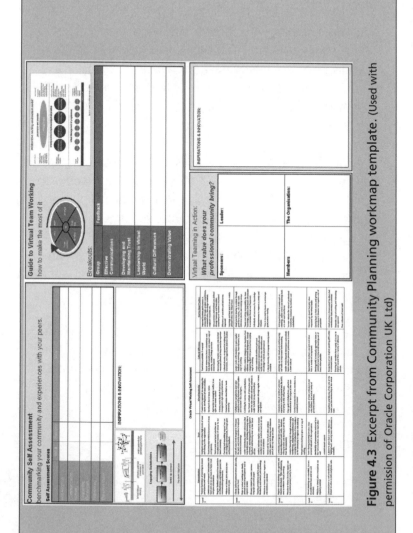

Figure 4.3 Excerpt from Community Planning workmap template. (Used with permission of Oracle Corporation UK Ltd)

- a self-assessment tool which they could share more widely within their professional community to propagate a vision of 'what good looks like';

- a record of the capabilities within their network of fellow PC leaders, captured in the River Diagram;

- experience of sharing and learning together as a community of PC leaders; and

- newly found skills in raft-building!

The approach was somewhat different in UK regional government offices.

Story 5 – Assessing Knowledge Management in UK Regional Government Offices

It started in late 2005 when a request appeared on the 'Learning to Fly' Yahoo! Group on the Internet.

Hi All

I work in a large (4,000 people) UK Government department. We are currently planning a series of 18 Knowledge management (KM) self-assessment workshops (across our 9 English regional offices). We have had a couple of trial runs and have decided to bring in a professional facilitator for the workshops.

Can anyone recommend a facilitator for the workshops, which will be based on the KM self-assessment stuff in learning to fly?

Many thanks!

Joe

The Government Office network consists of nine regional offices located in major cities across England. Government Offices (GOs) offer experience, expertise and regional feedback to Whitehall departments in both the development of policy and in the way that policies are best implemented. They are the primary means by which a wide range of government policies and programmes are delivered in the English regions. GOs represent 11 central government departments, and are involved in regenerating communities, fighting crime, tackling housing needs, improving public health, raising standards in education and skills, tackling countryside issues and reducing unemployment.

We responded to this request and helped tailor a self-assessment to their needs in order to measure their KM Competencies. The GOs found self-assessment particularly relevant because:

- they recognised that effective learning emerged from the strengths of groups and from their collaboration with partners;

- they could make use of their own knowledge and experience, and adapt that of others, so that everyone shared knowledge to improve performance;

- they realised that everyone has something to share and everyone has something to learn; and

- they found that assessing yourself is more subjective but leads to commitment to improve.

On a cold winter's day in early 2006 we held a self-assessment workshop with 17 staff from the Government Office for the North West (GONW), which has offices in Manchester and Liverpool. We asked the local KM champion to brief the participants individually before the event. The idea of a self-assessment workshop was unfamiliar to most of the staff, hence it was really important that they understood the intent and the process – and that they wanted to participate.

The representatives were selected carefully to ensure that a there was a good mix of staff at different grades and from different departments. We wanted to avoid having any highly disruptive cynics in the workshop, but at the same time we still wanted a lively debate. Local knowledge of these participants was key. Everyone spoke up and everyone had their say. There were differing views in the room, mainly due to different department practices, but they found it easy to resolve their overall score. The conversation drew out strengths in each other and the different departments shared their experiences of managing knowledge.

The physical environment wasn't great! A major building refurbishment was going on and we met in a stark meeting room on one of the empty upper floors, with scaffolding around the windows, and the occasional curious builder peering in! At the same time, a lot of organisational change was happening; as the organisation moved away from operational activities towards more strategic analysis, there was a focus on partnerships and collaboration. Undoubtedly all of this contributed to feelings of insecurity.

On the positive side, at the top of the hierarchy was a Regional Director who was looking for a profound change in behaviour and culture, and saw KM as something which could help bring about the change he was seeking. Keith Barnes, the Regional Director said:

> As an office specialising in knowing and understanding the regions, GONW's aim is to ensure that government policies and programmes are delivered effectively. And, like every organisation and business in today's ever-changing world, the challenge is to deliver more and do it with less resources.

> We had a look at how we could do this without jeopardising the vital role we play in the lives of 'our' people in the North West. And with the abundance of knowledge and talent among our staff an obvious answer was to generate an environment in which we all share our experiences, our enthusiasm and good practice to continually improve the way we work.

That leadership led to the directors repeating the exercise the following month to show commitment to the process. They grasped the five practices of KM quickly and were happy to assess themselves. The conversation led to a focus on networking to make Local Area Agreements work. They also saw that they needed a change in their leadership style.

They then compared their own assessment with what their staff had assessed and the differences between departments. There was also a brief comparison with other regional GOs. However since no GO had assessed themselves higher than level three in any practice, the scope for learning from elsewhere within the network was limited. This provoked further discussion about where they could learn from.

Demonstrating their commitment to improve, the directors agreed that they would speak to colleagues not able to attend and engage them. They would also address their staff on what they had learned.

A clear focus for building capability out of these two workshops emerged. The GONW leadership team focused on building their networks and partnerships for four of the key strategic themes, namely Obesity, Community Coherence & Diversity, Anti Social Behaviour and Worklessness. The vision of the leadership team was to enhance the quality of agreements they were negotiating with local government, introducing knowledge management techniques such as Peer Assist, After Action Reviews (AARs) and the creation of 'knowledge assets' (distilled collections of learning, Q&A, key documents and contacts) to support each theme. In particular they wanted to introduce Communities of Practice in order to encourage the sharing of good practices across the GONW which would lead to improved performance. They wanted to see that people felt more connected, were learning from others' experiences and reaching targets in less time while improving the quality of the results.

At the end of the year we conducted a retrospective review of what had happened during the year. Here are some of the key lessons about the approach that the GONW office shared with the other regional offices:

'It's not about a core team doing KM to you, but facilitators connecting you to teams that have tried something similar that may help you deliver your objectives.'

'It is not an event or a two month project. It's about a way of working, it's how we do things – connect, collaborate and learn.'

'Start where the energy is as some people naturally achieve this way of working. Perhaps it's more important to get people with enthusiasm than to hit all the right topics. Then they can reinforce the value with their peers, rather than having a consultant tell them.'

'It is about personal relationships and informal networking, picking up the phone and talking to people about it.'

'Facilitators have an important role to ensure everyone has their say.'

'Make the process clear and simple. Get clarity of what is in it for people to attend. Get the communication right for the invite so that the participants are clear on purpose and the amount of preparation required.'

One lesson which we would add is: 'Ensure that there is continuity between the participants in the self-assessment workshop, and the people who will lead the resulting actions.' We found when we ran the self-assessment workshop in January, when there was a good level of enthusiasm among the participants, they wanted to do more with it. However, when it came to the building of specific networks, there were a number of new people involved who had no knowledge of the self-assessment process or KM approaches. A consequence of this was that we had to spend more time explaining what it was all about, and less time transferring the capability to facilitate various KM techniques to staff in the office. In hindsight if the same champions from the various departments had stayed with the process throughout, the GONW would probably have a core of capable KM facilitators.

(Story included with thanks to the Government Office of the North West.)

Finally, a story which extends the use of a self-assessment tool beyond the boundaries of an organisation and into its supply chain.

Story 6 – Linking the Supply Chain

Nationwide is the largest building society in the world, the UK's third largest mortgage lender and the second largest savings provider, choosing to operate as a mutual rather than a public limited company. With around 1000 retail outlets and 20 000 employees, its portfolio of offices and branches requires a significant amount of support service, all of which is delivered through its 'Business Services' department (BSD).

Business Services manages a diverse supply chain, including project managers and shopfitters for branch refurbishment, building maintenance, ATM provision, office security, office move planning, catering and facilities management.

In 2004, Nationwide announced a £300 million investment in its retail network to upgrade its high street outlets and other access channels. This refurbishment programme represented a significant amount of business for the shopfitters within the supply chain. Rather than enter a traditional competitive bidding process, Tim Plummer, Head of Business Services, decided to use the existing regionally based supply chain and challenged them to collaborate and share knowledge: learn from each other and Nationwide. A lot of this was built on trust, for example, no contracts were put in place. The group of five main shopfitting suppliers accepted the challenge, and collaborated closely and successfully on all aspects of the refurbishment programme, finding a way to ensure that 'everybody wins'.

The success of this collaboration did not go unnoticed by other suppliers to Nationwide, and their success stories, shared at annual Supply Chain Conferences had a contagious effect; soon everyone was clear that Nationwide expected more than a simple supply chain. It was looking for an intelligent *supplier network*.

Since this time, the Nationwide team in Business Services have worked increasingly to encourage the supplier companies to work together, and with less day-to-day involvement from the building society.

Lynne Keech, internal knowledge consultant in Business Services Department picks up the story:

> We need to do more managing and less doing ourselves – the real expertise was in our suppliers, so we needed to make the best use of it, and do less 'doing' ourselves. However, to be confident that that would work, we needed them to work together as a team. We wanted to ensure that the linkages in the supply chain were really working. After all, who would want to rely on a chain where the links don't support each other!

> To help that happen, we needed them to really understand who we are, what we're about. We needed to get them involved and tap into their ideas. How can they help us to be better, how can their expertise help us to save money?

In keeping with this desire to involve the supply chain, and encourage them to be proactive with ideas and suggestions, a group of 10 representatives of supplier companies met to produce a self-assessment tool, to respond to the question 'What are the key practices required to be a successful partner to Nationwide?'

The group agreed on the following nine practices, and constructed a self-assessment tool with five levels for each practice:

- People management and development

- Communication

- Relationship management

- Learning and continuous improvement

- Innovation

- Sustainability

- Risk management

- Effective purchasing

- Financials and Management Information Reporting.

Having built and tested the self-assessment with a sample of their suppliers, Lynne then sent a request via e-mail to the entire supply chain, asking them to use the assessment and provide their scores, so that a River Diagram could be prepared and shared with all of the participants.

Since 2003 Nationwide Business Services has had a tradition of holding an annual conference with all key members of their supply chain. This is an opportunity for communication, feedback and networking, awards – and a chance for the supply chain to make requests of Nationwide and become involved in projects. What better opportunity to reveal the River Diagram and encourage well-informed networking between the suppliers, based on their strengths and weaknesses?

This is the request that Lynne sent out.

Improving Performance by Benchmarking and Sharing what we Know

We would like you to participate in a performance improvement benchmarking exercise. All attendees at the forthcoming Supply Chain Conference will be involved. Please read on to find out more.

Why are we doing this?

The purpose of this self-assessment is to measure your organisation against a number of key management capabilities with the intention of making real improvement. This is not just a measurement exercise, it is about suppliers sharing what they know and improving because they are all using the same measures. The capabilities matrix was put together collaboratively by Business Services and a number of our suppliers including Rocare, Turner & Townsend, Barnwood, Mitie, Alfred McAlpine and Principio.

We believe that everyone has something to share and everyone has something to learn. So please be candid in your discussions and honest in your scoring – everyone else will be!

How will this be undertaken?

You will find below a matrix with nine capabilities. Each capability has five levels, ranging from Level 1 (basic) up to Level 5 (expert/experienced). You/your team should review each capability and decide which statement best describes your organisation. I have included a worked example.

Step-by-Step Guide

- Print off this document

- Take a look at the worked examples

- Then review the self-assessment

- You will be recording your scores in the Excel spreadsheet (attached to e-mail)

- Sit down with key employees dispersed across your organisation that know it well

- Start with one capability

- Read the statement at Level 1

- If your organisation is this good or better, then move up to Level 2 and so on

- Record the score that best describes where your company is

- Do this for each capability

- This should give you nine scores (no half scores please)

- Then, think about which three capabilities you most wish to improve over the next 12 months. These are your priorities

- Once you have chosen three (no more!) decide how much you want to improve the three priorities by

- Record your three target scores for these priority areas (again on the spreadsheet)

- Finally, identify three capabilities that you wish to share – the reason: because you have something to offer

What Next?

We will be collating the results and publishing them at the forthcoming Supply Chain Conference. The way we publish the results will clearly show for each capability who wants to improve and who has something to share. We will then be encouraging people to share what they do and how they do it, that way everyone can learn and improve and everyone wins.

The resulting River Diagram, which was presented at the Supply Chain Conference, showed a wide range of capability levels (see Figure 4.4). For effective purchasing and relationship management, the range of capabilities spanned the entire river. This indicated that there was plenty of potential for sharing and learning. Figure 4.4 shows that Supplier X was

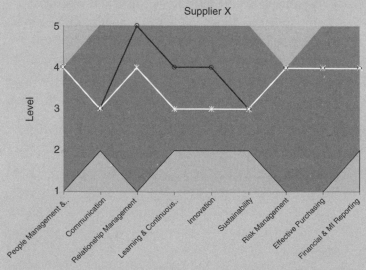

Click on the practice text to see who you can share with

Figure 4.4 Supply Chain River Diagram. (Used with permission of Nationwide Building Society)

one of the organisations seeking to improve their performance in Relationship management, Learning and continuous improvement and Innovation.

Unfortunately for the suppliers, although the River Diagram indicated plenty of potential for sharing and learning, the action-packed conference agenda didn't allow plenty of time!

Recognising this, Lynne organised a separate 'Peer Assist' day one month later where representatives from the suppliers came with clear ideas of their strengths and areas for improvement. The data from the self-assessment enabled Lynne to allocate the participants to a mix of table discussions in which they could give and receive knowledge.

Today, two years after the creation of the supply chain self-assessment, a number of work themes (project teams comprising Nationwide staff and suppliers) have picked up and formalised the work from some of these Peer Assist sessions, so knowledge-sharing lives on.

Lynne concludes:

> Creating the self-assessment and then involving all our suppliers in generating the River diagram were really important steps for us. They helped our supply chain to appreciate just how much potential for learning and sharing was there, and to make more connections with their peers. We started the journey with a supply chain, and are now much closer to our goal of creating an innovative supplier network.

Launching and Going to Scale

So what are the practical steps in getting started and going to scale? It is more than just a single meeting; rather, it is a journey of improvement. For many participants it will be a change of approach; a different way of thinking about issues, a different way of working.

Here are the key steps, from our experience.

1. First get a group of knowledgeable people together to create a draft self-assessment. This provides the framework and the boundaries for a conversation, and it creates a common language for people to meaningfully share what they know, and what great performance looks like.

2. Ensure they test the self-assessment on themselves first, and then with others in a variety of different settings. If it was constructed at head office then make sure you try it in field locations or overseas offices – somewhere away from the 'ivory tower'!

3. Collect feedback on the practices and content of the levels. Establish whether the users were able to have the conversations they wanted to have, and whether they identified their strengths and areas to improve.

4. Ensure that you communicate the relevance, purpose and what is the incentive for the group to spend time doing a self-assessment.

Be aware that if you request people you have not met before to assess themselves they may treat you with suspicion. Is their job at risk if they don't answer it correctly? Will funding stop, or be diverted to those reporting higher scores? You will have much more cooperation if you work through people who have existing relationships with the target group. In a development scenario, this might be the local NGO representative; in an organisation it might be a credible champion located in the regional office.

5. Revise the self-assessment framework according to the feedback you get until such time as the suggested changes start flipping backwards and forwards – someone is suggesting you change back something you changed last week to what it was. Adopt a Wikipedia approach to developing the content and accept that the wording will never be perfect; the right framework is the one that most people agree on. You might consider using a Wiki to revise the self-assessment, but keep an eye on what is changing, and whether the participants of the original workshop are engaged in any Wiki discussions.

6. Conduct local and regional workshops. Start where the reception is most positive and work towards the most cynical. Gain ownership of the self-assessment, perhaps through the dream exercise outlined earlier in this chapter, so that people are comfortable with the range of practices and the levels for each practice, from basic to high.

7. Encourage participants to apply it to their own part of the organisation.

   It is best not to facilitate the self-assessment for others until you have assessed your own group.

8. Organisations should use impartial facilitators to ensure everyone's experience is heard and understood, and that people own the outcome. The facilitators should keep the focus of the conversation on sharing experiences not opinions.

9. Secure commitment to use the different way of working and thinking in ongoing projects. Don't portray it as a brand new initiative requiring resources and funding; rather, position it as a shift in approach from 'providing a response' to revealing the strengths that others already have to apply to the issue. Discuss with participants how they might continue to communicate between face-to-face sessions. This might be by phone, e-mail, social networking tools, etc. Peers sharing with each other can be a great source of support and encouragement. Organise a regular rhythm of events to keep the momentum going and the energy levels topped up. People are more likely to get into action if they have to report progress and share examples with their peers when they meet. The approach is a change in the way of thinking and working, not a one-off event.

10. Encourage the participants to stop and reflect frequently so that they learn from what they are doing.

After 18 months or two years of regional events hold a big jamboree, a 'knowledge fair', across the region, or even at global scale to share what they have achieved in the different regions. This will make people feel good about their achievements and build further momentum. The participants will learn from others' insights and problems shared. It will also build relationships face-to-face which can then be sustained into the future by providing a collaboration space for people to continue the conversations with people they have learned to trust.

11. By now the network will have formed a life of its own, but it would be smart to put another date in the diary for a year hence to check on progress. This will reinforce the expectation that they are in a journey of improvement, and keep the momentum going. You might find that capability has built to such a level that there will be a need to extend level five (See Chapter 8). This is a cause for celebration, but we should never stop learning to improve.

I can still recall the wise observation of a schoolgirl in Zambia; 'We are at level five on this practice but we still have much to learn!'

This is the longest chapter in the book, but necessarily so. By now we feel you will not only understand the approach, but have the confidence to use it in your own organisation.

The Role of the Facilitator

Facilitation is key to success with this approach. To create the right conversation and give everyone the chance to speak and be listened to, needs someone to take care of the conversation process. What is a facilitator and what exactly do they do?

If we look for a dictionary definition of the verb 'to facilitate' we find it is 'to make an action or process easy or easier'. So a facilitator is someone who enables groups and organisations to take action more easily together, to collaborate and achieve synergy. A facilitator's role is to make it easier for the group to arrive at its own answer, decision or result. A facilitator is 'content neutral', that is, doesn't offer his or her own opinions. They assist the group in achieving a consensus so that it has a strong basis for collaborative action. The role can be considered like that of a midwife who assists in the process of delivery but is certainly not the producer of the baby!

We can consider a continuum between coaching, facilitating and training. Coaching is one-on-one. For example,

I often find myself talking to the meeting sponsor in the breaks to get them to change their attitude. If they are looking for a group decision but already have the answer in mind then the environment is not conducive to the free flow of ideas and collaboration on possible responses.

At the other end of the continuum, training may be appropriate when the level of capability in the room for a particular topic is not high, in which case the appropriate intervention is to introduce some content. In between is the activity of facilitating a group to reach its desired outcome.

What Are the Attributes of a Good Facilitator?

According to Wikipedia, the basic skills of a facilitator are to encourage good meeting practices – practices such as:

- timekeeping;

- following an agreed-upon agenda; and

- keeping a clear record of key decisions and commitments so that the meeting achieves its desired outcome.

To those basic skills we would add:

- flexibility to manage the group dynamics;

- good listening skills, including ability to ask the right questions;

- paraphrasing;

- quoting verbatim when emphasising a point;

- managing a queue of comments and questions on a topic;

- drawing people out; and

- giving everyone the opportunity to say what they have to contribute.

Facilitators respect what people have to say and appreciate the strengths in people to tackle the issue at hand. They work by invitation, not by imposition. Sometimes several facilitators work together in a team approach, supporting each other, and reflecting together before, during and after the meeting.

What Does a Facilitator Do?

Facilitation can take place at several levels and depends upon how much intervention is required and how clear people are on the outcome to be achieved. The methods and techniques required must be tailored accordingly. Sometimes the only requirement is to capture the key decisions and action points, in other words scribing with a flipchart pen. Sometimes clarity of the desired outcome only emerges through conversation, so plenty of help is required to create that meaningful conversation.

Our experience is that at least 60% of facilitation is in the preparation, yet all too frequently the facilitator is only brought in, or nominated, at the start of the meeting.

It is important to understand your sponsor's expectations beforehand. Note that this may not be the person who contacts you to ask if you are available. Track down the person whose meeting it really is and if you are not sure, look for the one who is 'on the hook' for delivering something.

We frequently use four simple questions to elicit expectations:

What is your desired outcome?
What is currently on people's minds that will affect how they respond?
Can you get to your desired outcome from what is on people's minds?
Can you be satisfied with less than your desired outcome?

Ask as many individual participants as possible to share their expectations and objectives before the group meets; often these are different from the sponsor's. Balance these inputs with the draft agenda, and if you are unable to address any expectations in the meeting, say so, and deal with them by explaining when and how they will be addressed.

At the start of the meeting define the role of partici-pants. In the case of self-assessment, we don't want any observers and everyone is a participant. To build on the earlier baseball analogy, we want people to be 'on the field' rather than 'in the stands'. Define your own role as facilitator so everyone is clear. Help the group to decide what ground rules it will follow and remind participants of these when they are not followed.

Working as a facilitator, we would also expect to:

- Write down the desired outcome and deliverables of the meeting or workshop and remind the group of them when they get off track.

- Keep the group on course to achieve its goals in the time allotted.

- Create an environment where participants feel comfortable participating freely; give everyone a voice.

- Ask open-ended questions that stimulate thinking.

- Guide the group through processes designed to help them listen to each other and create solutions together; have a variety of methods and tools to use creatively in difficult moments for facilitating people and groups.

- Offer a possible wording for an unspoken question or issue.

- Capture actions and decisions in a large script on the wall for all to see and ensure they are assigned to individuals with a timescale. I prefer to include a noun and a verb to make a complete sentence. Use the test: 'Will this be understandable next week?'

Alternatively nominate a recorder – a person, preferably with a computer and projector – so participants have the opportunity to read and endorse or disagree with what is captured.

- Summarise what has been agreed and achieved at the end of a session and at the end of the meeting.

Typically a meeting has bouts of divergence and convergence, often emerging in ways which were not programmed into the agenda. Most people start on a new topic by offering ideas, solutions, opinions and past experiences. Some will settle on solutions fast while others are still exploring ideas or thinking over what others have shared. A problem usually arises when people converge on a decision or solution at different times. At this point, we often enter a painful period where people cannot figure out what is going on. Some participants get frustrated and irritated, some wait patiently believing they will get their chance to speak.

Sam Kaner *et al.* in their useful workbook, *The Facilitator's Guide to Participatory Decision Making*, call this the 'Groan Zone'. Just to acknowledge the existence of this Groan Zone can be a significant and helpful step for participants to take. Don't avoid contention because it sometimes leads to important breakthroughs. We like to think of it as putting the effort where the energy is. If there is immediate agreement and little energy associated with the agreement, then you could find that the group are taking the route of least resistance and maintaining the status quo. Better solutions may become apparent when different viewpoints are explored.

What is the Outcome of a Well Facilitated Meeting?

There are three reasons for using a facilitator to help run a meeting. As a consequence of using a facilitator, the group should be able to:

- tap into broader thinking;

- gain buy-in for decisions and actions agreed; and

- make better decisions.

Let me share a recent example which demonstrates what I mean by 'creating an environment where participants feel comfortable sharing ideas and experiences'.

I was in the District of Karnataka, India working with a group of local charities or non-governmental organisations (NGOs) and we were learning from each other. Together we visited three villages close to the district of Bellary, with whom the charities had good working relationships. They were providing information and education about HIV, educating villagers on topics such as: how it is spread, how to avoid it and how to deal with the consequences. Their sponsors were directing their effort to protecting vulnerable young women.

We encouraged them to try a different way of working. We visited the three villages to listen and learn what the issues and concerns were and what they were already doing to respond to them. On the fourth day we brought together representatives from the three villages, including village elders, young women and young men, to share their experiences in their own villages (Figure 5.1). This

Figure 5.1 Village discussion.

was something that hadn't happened before. Indeed the different groups had not discussed the impact of HIV and AIDS together in their own villages before that week.

We mixed the groups up and asked them to tackle different issues in small groups comprising about 10 people. They sat in circles on the floor of the village hall where we were meeting. A local NGO representative was assigned to each group. The discussion was held in the local language. I was unable to follow the discussion, so I observed the interactions within the circles. In one group it was apparent that the conversation was following a pattern – first between one of the group and the NGO representative, and then another of the group and the representative, and so on. The representative was providing all the answers, like the hub of a wheel. I intervened. Through an interpreter I explained that the role of the NGO person was not to train, educate or provide the answers but to encourage the group to share their own responses and experiences. Despite my explanation, it still wasn't working and the third time I intervened it was to physically remove the NGO representative from the circle! I asked her to stand with me on the other side of the hall and watch what happened. The circle closed up and the conversation restarted. Suddenly the dynamics changed completely – the conversation flowed across and back around the circle, first in one direction, and then another. People who had so far made no contribution were making their voice heard. It became animated, there was laughter and everyone participated in the sharing and learning.

Her eyes lit up. The light bulb flashed – now she understood what I had been trying to explain! She went back and joined the circle as a listener – and learned things she had not heard before.

My role, despite not understanding a word they were saying, was to create an environment where participants felt comfortable sharing ideas and experiences.

So we can apply the approach and have a good facilitator. Now how do we visualise the results?

Creating the River

6

So far in the book we have explored how to work with a group to create a self-assessment framework and how best to facilitate its use, so that the conversations flow. The River Diagram is a powerful way to illustrate the sources of good practice amongst the groups completing the self-assessment, and to stimulate the transfer of knowledge and good practices.

Let's say that you have the results of some self-assessment scores, and want to take the next step. This chapter looks at the practicalities of how you go about creating a River Diagram – using a computer, flipcharts, a field, or sitting on the roof of a houseboat, floating on a river!

If you look at Excel, you won't find 'River chart' as one of the standard choices of charts, along with pie charts and histograms which you can create from the menu. Visualising performance data in this way is becoming increasingly popular, but not sufficiently so for the Microsoft developers in Redmond to build it in into their product.

If you are searching through the chart gallery in Excel, and looking for a comparison, then the Radar chart is similar in concept. In effect, it's a River Diagram which is wrapped around in a circle. The only difficulty is that interpreting it makes your head spin – literally!

Technology isn't a prerequisite for using a River Diagram. Geoff helped apply the approach to the fight against AIDS in a number of countries around the world, in some cases where there was no electricity! Pieces of string can be used to mark out the boundaries of a river, and a Stairs Diagram can be easily built with a number of sheets of paper stuck to the wall or even a pad of post-it notes. Even if you do have technology at your disposal, you might consider a low-tech approach – it can lead to a greater understanding and sense of involvement – and better conversations.

Constructing the River Diagram on Paper

Some people understand the River Diagram right away, while others freeze like rabbits in the headlight of a car! Not everyone thinks visually, hence it is helpful go back to first principles and involve people in constructing it on flip chart paper.

We start by drawing a 10 by 5 grid – the 10 practices along the top and the five levels of competence up the vertical (Figure 6.1). People then mark their assessed scores on the grid, so if they are level one on practice one they mark the bottom left hand grid. In Thailand I've seen this done with rubber bands taped on the grid with

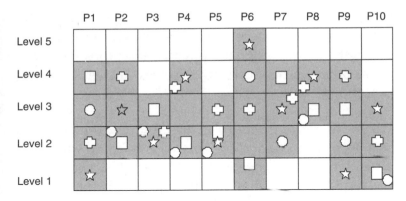

Figure 6.1 Creating a River Diagram on Paper.

a different colour for each group. In India they used different coloured stickies. You can be as creative as you like!

In the example in Figure 6.1 four groups have placed their current levels for each of 10 practices, a different symbol for each group.

When each group has put up their mark for each practice, invite the whole group to stand near the picture, ask someone to draw around the 'envelope' of scores, encompassing the range between the lowest and the highest scores. They do this by joining the dots on the lowest scores for each practice and then joining the dots for the highest scores; these are the banks of the river. If you have a thick green marker pen available, you might colour these in to emphasise the point.

Pick out the scores for one group as an example. Where their score for a particular practice is near the highest scores of the group, this is a strength which they can share with other groups. Conversely where their score is amongst the lowest for the practice then they can learn from others who score themselves higher for that practice.

Where the range from low to high is great, then there is significant opportunity for the groups to share with each other. Where the range is small there is less opportunity to learn (although it is worth emphasising that if they have different experiences then it is still valuable for people on the same level to learn from each other). If there is a large 'north bank' at the top of the picture, then all groups may require some outside intervention or external input to help them build their competence.

To test their understanding, you might ask the group: 'If we are a learning organisation, what would we expect to happen to the shape of the river, over time?' Hopefully, someone will suggest that the river should move north-wards, and become narrower. To develop this point, you can play with the metaphor of 'eroding away the north bank' and 'laying up sediment on the south bank'; or turning a wide river into a narrow canal.

Innovative and Practical Ways to Visualise a River Diagram

Pushing the creative boundaries a little further, in Kithit-huni village in Uganda, Ian Campbell and others facili-tated a self-assessment in a village square without even the use of paper! People voted with their feet as to which level they thought their village was at for a particular practice of AIDS Competence. Some thought 'level five' and went to stand under the mango tree, others at level three stood by the first hut, those that thought level two were by an upturned bucket. There was much cheering and jeering as teams chose then reset their levels. Each openly discussed why they chose their levels. When everyone had decided on the level then those at level two called out a question to those at a higher level to learn how to become better at the practice. This worked particularly well because storytelling is the medium for sharing knowledge in Africa. Significantly however, this process has been repeated in places as far away as India, China and Bolivia with similar positive energy. The physical separation helped people realise the separation in competence. It was a noisy, chaotic, energetic session, and by the end everyone realised their different strengths and had improved some practices by sharing with others. Next time, there will be a crowd under that mango tree!

Claire Campbell and Bobby Zachariah of the Salvation Army conducted one self-assessment on a 40-foot houseboat cruising down a river in Kerala in Southern India. A network of about 30 facilitators from many parts of India gathered to discuss stimulating local community response. Bobby arranged a 'day off' which in itself was unusual! They felt it appropriate to 'relax' with an introduction to the self-assessment tool. During the course of a six-hour cruise they held a captive audience! They discussed strengths in small groups and shared experiences, then came together to plot the River Diagram on the roof of the boat. What could be more appropriate? A show of hands around the deck of the boat was sufficient to connect sharers with learners. The response from the participants was enthusiastic, sustained despite the intense heat, and revitalising for most of them.

Having helped to construct the River Diagram on a flip chart, people are inevitably 'wowed' when they see how it can be automated in Excel and clamour for a copy! Not only does the spreadsheet do all of the work for you, but it enables you to flip quickly between the scores of different groups, and see how they compare for each practice. The Excel tool also automatically creates the Stairs Diagrams so that the groups can see who to share with and who to learn from for each practice, showing the supply and demand.

The instructions for building the diagram in Excel are straightforward, and are provided in Appendix C. However, if you don't want to build your own Excel model, take a look at www.nomoreconsultants.org for some downloadable examples and templates to get you started.

Creating the Stairs Diagram

Again, because the Stairs Diagram is a visual model, it is often best to prepare paper copies so that people can interact and reference it on a wall in the meeting room. Here are the 'tangram' puzzle instructions!

Take three sheets of A4 paper – green, yellow and red – fold each sheet into six squares as shown and prepare a Stairs Diagram as in Figure 6.2. Prepare one for each practice.

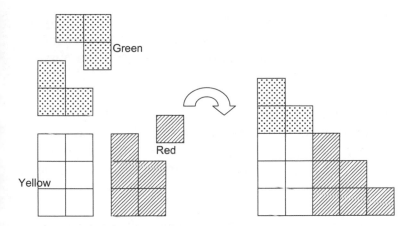

Figure 6.2 Creating the Stairs Diagram.

So for 10 practices you will require 10 sheets of yellow paper, 10 of red and five of green. The final composite will fit neatly onto a sheet of flipchart paper.

Once you have your set of stairs, encourage people to write their names in the appropriate square for each practice. The square they select will be the intersection of their current score and the size of the gap between that score and their target. If their current score is level three, and they want to improve by two levels over a defined time period, move your finger from the third square up in the first column two columns to the right. It should now be in the top red square, exactly half-way up the stairs. You'll probably need to give an example, showing how the scores on a self-assessment relate to the stairs, just to make sure that everyone understands.

If you are poetically or musically inclined, and the group is receptive to a light-hearted approach, you might even share with them the well loved A.A. Milne poem, *Halfway down the stairs*, in which Milne describes Christopher Robin's temporary seat as being neither 'in the nursery' nor 'in the town'.

You could challenge them that, all too often, half-way up the stairs is where we choose to stop, and explore the reasons for that. Is it safer to stick with the crowd to avoid the sometimes unwanted attention which being at the top or the bottom can bring?

If you know your participants well, and their taste in entertainment, then take a look on YouTube (or follow the link on www.nomoreconsultants.org) for the endearing video of Muppets star, Kermit the Frog's nephew, Robin, singing it. My children loved it anyway!

The following story from the National Health Service in England illustrates the use of the River and Stairs Diagrams with larger groups.

Story 7 – Developing a Knowledge Culture in the National Health Service

For some years, knowledge management activities have been observed in different parts of the National Health Service (NHS), with many different applications in both clinical and management practice. However it was recognised that unless the underlying culture of the NHS was receptive and supportive to the development of knowledge management, then many of these initiatives were doomed to failure.

In March 2008 a report (Hill Review) issued by the NHS Institute for Innovation and Improvement (England) recommended that:

> In every NHS organisation someone at board level should be entrusted with the role of Chief Knowledge Officer for that organisation ...

The role of the Chief Knowledge Officer (CKO) would include a requirement:

> To steer the development of a knowledge management (KM) strategy for their organisation, ... The KM strategy needs to be aligned with organisational strategy, and needs to address, amongst other things, developing the organisational culture.

> To lead the development, management and sharing of knowledge within NHS and partner organisations to maximise its use in supporting the improvement of Patient Care.

In most instances the CKO would be an additional role for the member of the board, rather than being a new post. There was no prescription as to which member of the board that should be, simply that they should be:

> Passionate about the importance of making full use of an organisation's knowledge for the benefit of patient care and service improvement.

Fully understanding of the complementary nature and value of data, information, research evidence and experience.

Committed to creating and sustaining a knowledge-sharing culture by actively seeking to remove the boundaries of departmental and professional silos.

Committed to the learning and development of all staff, thereby developing the organisation's knowledge.

By the early summer of 2008, around one third of all NHS organisations in England had identified a board member to take on the CKO role. From this group, two questions kept arising:

What did they need to do to develop the KM strategy and to develop the culture?

What were other organisations doing?

At this point it was decided to link the support for the development of the CKO role to another piece of work that was already looking at knowledge-sharing in NHS organisations. A self-assessment and River Diagram workshop approach was being used with local groups to enable participating organisations to:

• identify their organisation's knowledge management strengths and weaknesses;

- identify two areas of knowledge management practice to focus development on;

- reflect, share ideas and learn from each other.

The workshop included the completion of a 'knowledge management and organisation development' self-assessment questionnaire, adapted for use in the NHS, from the tool included in *Learning to Fly*. This is included in Appendix D.

A national workshop for NHS CKOs was held in the autumn of 2008. The aim of the event was to support CKOs in leading the development, management and sharing of knowledge within their organisation; and to gain their input to the shaping of future developments and the establishment of CKO networks. A key part of the agenda was to introduce the CKOs to the self-assessment tool, as a means of learning more about their own organisation and as a means of getting them to start to learn and share with each other. However, with over 130 participants in the workshop, the prospect of capturing their scores 'live' during the workshop and representing them on a River Diagram was unrealistic. Firstly, the time required to collect and process the results would have created a frustrating delay, and secondly, with 130 sets of data, it is statistically likely that the spread of scores in this large sample will create a very broad river – potentially a wide straight-sided canal!

Rachel Cooke, fellow at the NHS Institute for Improvement and Innovation, decided to focus on the use of the Stairs Diagrams as a potential marketplace for sharing, and to generate the River Diagrams after the event, clustering the scores into regional groupings which represented the 10 Strategic Health Authorities (SHAs) in England.

> We wanted to capture the individual scores, so we gave everybody a copy of the self-assessment with a carbon-paper backing. The CKOs reflected on the words, and recorded their current scores and targets. We wanted the day to be dynamic, and help the CKOs to discover the help which was available to them from their peers. Ultimately we wanted the day to be the start of a CKO network.

Rachel and her team printed a series of Stairs Diagrams on large posters – each one around two metres across, representing each of the eight practices. These were positioned prominently on the walls around the conference room. Having completed their self-assessment, the CKOs then got to their feet and wrote their name in the relevant box on each of the staircases. This done, it was then easy to identify the practices which were the improvement priorities for the greatest number of CKOs. With the potential supply and demand now visible, a high-speed sharing exercise followed, with the participants taking turns to gather around the Stairs Diagrams for which they had most energy to share or learn about, spending three 15-minute sessions at different staircases in the resulting 'knowledge marketplace'.

Rachel concludes:

> This part was a bit chaotic at times, perhaps too chaotic for some of the participants. However, it was a powerful

illustration to everybody of the potential energy for sharing in the network. Our challenge now is to ensure that these connections and conversations continue as the national CKO network develops, and that in parallel, the regional SHA River Diagrams support a more local approach to sharing and learning.

In reading this chapter so far, we hope you can see how visualising those with strengths and those who have something to learn can stimulate connections and collaboration and that you have picked up a sense of the energy that the River Diagram can generate. Whether you use the logical power of Excel, the informality of flipcharts, enhance the session with music and poetry – or even get outside and use physical space – you'll create a buzz for your participants.

Now, how many performance improvement workshops have you experienced, about which you can say that?

One possible explanation for the buzz comes from psychologist and author Howard Gardner. In the 1980s, he pioneered the idea of multiple intelligences. He identified seven different kinds of intelligence, each one lending itself to a different learning style:

- Linguistic

- Logical-mathematical

- Musical

- Visual-spatial

- Kinaesthetic

- Interpersonal and

- Intrapersonal.

Gardner suggests that we each possess all seven of the above intelligences to a greater or lesser degree. In principle, a well-designed learning event will address several of these intelligences to maximise the overall levels of engagement in a group. The combination of self-assessment (Linguistic and Interpersonal) and the River and Stairs Diagrams (Logical-mathematical, Visual-spatial, Interpersonal, potentially Kinaesthetic – and even Musical if you include Robin the Frog's song!) should engage the learning styles of all of your participants.

Having engaged the group in the potential for learning, how do you then capitalise on this enthusiasm and mobilise the learning? The next chapter gets us 'learning from experience'.

Learning from Experience

7

Do you remember arranging your first date?

Can you feel the butterflies in your stomach as you try to persuade your dry mouth to ask 'that question'? Can you sense the fear of rejection, sudden vulnerability to rejection and ridicule in front of your schoolmates?

What if she says no? What if I've misread everything? What if I missed my opportunity?

Why couldn't someone have invented texting or instant messaging in 1982, and given me an easier method, and a less public rejection!

You'd like to think that connecting the supply and demand for knowledge in an organisation would be straightforward compared to the complexities and insecurities of adolescent romance, but it's not always the case. At least we had the benefit of active hormones to help us overcome our embarrassment.

This chapter explores:

- Using 'Offers and Requests' to connect supply and demand.

- Sharing amongst equals – the Peer Assist process.

- You can lead a horse to the river, but can you make it drink?

- Recognising and overcoming four syndromes which prevent knowledge-sharing.

As you will have read in the earlier chapters, self-assessment is an excellent way to provoke valuable conversations within teams, as they share experiences and discuss examples of their level of competence relative to a particular self-assessment framework. Provoking valuable conversations *between* teams however, is another matter, and yet these conversations are often the ones which lead people to a solution. The Stairs Diagram, which is derived from the River Diagram, is a great way to visualise who has something to share and who has a desire to learn about a particular topic.

Posting these diagrams somewhere where people can gather around them physically or virtually is a great stimulus for sharing.

BP used a complementary approach to create connections between business units, an open process of Offers and Requests.

Offers and Requests

Once a team or department had completed a self-assessment process and identified their current scores and targets for improvement, BP required one further small step to be taken, entitled 'Offers and Requests'. Each business unit was asked to make three offers of help – practices which they had scored highly in, and were willing to share with other business units.

These are two examples of offers from BP business units:

> Practice: Manage Contractors and Third Parties Effectively. We have extensive experience in this area as a result of a recent plant/business acquisition. We have a lot of lessons-learned to share regarding contract and cost control. Note that these lessons-learned encompass both good and not-so-good experiences!

> Practice: Corrosion Management. We can offer examples of a risk-ranked comprehensive corrosion management system for pipeline integrity and process equipment and piping.

Each business unit was also asked to make three requests for help, based around the practices which they wanted to improve as a matter of priority.
For example:

> We want to raise our performance in managing spare parts from level two to level four this year.

We learned that the implied balance (three offers and three requests) worked well to help the engineers in BP overcome a macho reluctance to ask for help, as it was clear that all of their peers were asking for help at the same time. The sense of vulnerability associated with being the first to share was also diminished because each of their fellow business units was making three requests. The Offers and Requests (around 200 of each) were recorded centrally, where they were 'matched' and introduced by e-mail.

We allowed ourselves a smile as we sent out the matchmaking invitations. It took us back to those crumpled 'My friend fancies you ...' notes that used to get passed around under the school desks!

Offers and Requests don't need to be managed as a centrally coordinated process for a distributed community. They can also work well as an exercise in a group workshop using post-it notes and two flipcharts or areas on a wall.

Once people have written their Offers and Requests, and stuck them to the wall as a 'post-it gallery', encourage them to seek out someone with a 'match', and give them a short time (two to three minutes) to 'speed date' and exchange contact details, then move on to the next 'match'.

In the autumn of 2008, international agri-business Syngenta brought together 500 of its research scientists for a corporate conference where they used a creative variant of the post-it gallery. In place of the usual Post-it® notes and flipcharts, they strung a washing line across the meeting room and encouraged their employees to write their Offers and Requests on cut-out 'paper clothes'. Requests were written on the trousers, and offers on the T-shirt shapes. As the afternoon progressed, delegates became intrigued by the display and were inspired to write matching Offers and Requests, which were joined to their respective clothing counterparts on the washing line.

This made it clear to all that connections were being made, and drew a focus to the 'odd clothes'. The organising team collected in the washing at the end of the event, and used email to connect the various parties.

At conferences and major meetings, you might find yourself introducing a self-assessment tool to a large group, but you are unable to process their self-assessment results in real time, and lack the time and space for such washing-line creativity. Here's a simple way to increase the connections with such a group, just by using their name badges.

Simply colour-code the practices on the self-assessment and provide small sticky dots in each delegate pack which correlate with the coloured practices on the self-assessment. Having completed the self-assessment individually, ask the delegates to choose one or two practices for which they have an offer, and one or two request areas where they want to make an improvement. Place the sticky dots which correlate to the 'offer' in the top right hand corner of the badge, and the 'request dots' in the bottom corner and allocate the group 10 minutes to speed-network, find their matching halves and exchange details. The only difficulty with such a technique is

Figure 7.1 Offers and Requests washing line. (Copyright Syngenta. Photographer: Mark Howard)

re-establishing order in the room – hence it works particularly well just before a meal break, where the networking can continue naturally.

You will have noted from these examples that these matchmaking activities succeed when they are creative and light-hearted, and involve a level of physical mingling and social interaction.

However, for many groups you may not have the luxury of face-to-face interaction. This is where social networking and Web 2.0 tools have a contribution to make. Draw your inspiration from the ever-growing range of social networking tool such as Facebook, Twitter and Yammer which all give a sense of real-time status and encourage exchange.

Could you encourage your community to subscribe to a simple blog or wiki detailing Offers and Requests, with responses provided by comment or edit? Perhaps you could even stage a virtual matchmaking event in SecondLife?

Don't let the lack of physical interaction limit your creativity!

Hints and Tips for a Successful Exchange of Offers and Requests

- Start by asserting 'everyone has something to learn, everyone has something to share'.

- Label each Offer or Request with the practice they relate to. This will make it easier to cluster and match them later.

- Encourage people to express what they write as clear offers of help or requests for help, rather than bland statements. If appropriate, you could require that each sentence starts with 'I offer my experience in ...' or 'I am seeking help with ...'. Without this guidance, you may end up with one-word post-its which lack both the emotional hook and the detail to enable people to respond.

- Ensure all Offers and Requests have a name and contact details – e-mail and telephone.

- If possible, include a photograph of the person making the request or offer to add a personal touch.

- If it is part of a workshop process, apply some time pressure to enable as many connections as possible to be made. Maximise the available time to make multiple connections rather than get into the details – they can follow up later.

- If you are running a matchmaking process where the people are not physically present, send out the details of each match to the individuals concerned and make it the responsibility of the requestor to 'make the first move'. That way they won't both wait for each other.

- Consider sending PowerPoint 'invitations' which set up a meeting for the parties concerned. You could be creative and use embedded music – for example excerpts from 'Help!' by the Beatles. Adding novelty appeal may help it to stand out in an over-filled e-mail inbox.

- In cases where there are multiple offers of help which match a single request, it might be appropriate to set up a different form of meeting, such as a 'Peer Assist' or 'knowledge fair' to make effective use of time.

- Ask for feedback after a short time. Ask for examples and stories from people who have managed to follow up on their requests. Share a summary of these with the whole group to galvanise the laggards into action!

Let's return briefly to our example on 'Meeting Effectiveness'.

Imagine that the group looking at meeting effectiveness in Chapter 4 wanted to learn more about the decision-making process. Having completed the self-assessment, they recognised that they had a strength in defining the purpose and outcomes of a meeting. Having used a Stairs Diagram to establish who is already good at decision-making (and is willing to share what they know), they might request a meeting to share experience about practices of decision-making. What worked and what didn't work for others? By the end of the meeting they will all have a collection of tools, approaches and ideas to use and know when to apply each. They might even collectively combine successful parts from several positive experiences to develop a process which nobody has tried out before. These meetings can be sources of innovation as well as sources of shared experience.

Learning from Experience Through a Peer Assist

So far, in this chapter and the previous one we have illustrated a number of simple mechanisms for connecting sharers with learners, creating a marketplace for knowledge-sharing. We have looked at examples of modified name badges at a conference, playing cards, Offers and Requests washing lines, and a series of rapid small group exchanges at the 'foot of the stairs'. All of the examples so far have involved short exchanges, often little more than a 10-minute conversation, an exchange of contact details and perhaps an offer to follow up with more detail at a later stage.

Sometimes this is all that is required to get on the right track.

There are times though when the business need or topic merits a more in-depth discussion where a group of people can take the time and space required to share their experience in more detail, and to reflect together on what new possibilities could arise as a consequence. One way of running such a discussion is through a simple meeting structure known as a Peer Assist.

Peer Assists originated in BP in the mid 1990s and have since become a widely adopted method used by organisations to learn before doing. A Peer Assist is an event, meeting or workshop which brings peers (people working at a similar level) together to share their experiences, insights and knowledge on an identified challenge or problem.

We explained the technique in depth in Chapter 7 of *Learning to Fly*, so rather than repeat the detail here, we will explore the key principles.

1. It involves assistance.

    Firstly, a Peer Assist is focused on a specific challenge or problem. Someone requires assistance, and that someone has asked for help. They have made the request and are seeking input from others with experience.

2. It involves peers.

    Lord Browne, BP's CEO who championed the introduction of knowledge management to BP, stated in an interview for *Harvard Business Review*:

The politics accompanying hierarchies hampers the free exchange of knowledge. People are much more open with their peers. They are much more willing to share and to listen.

This is the reason that the participants in the most effective Peer Assists are working at a similar level. In the Nationwide story from Chapter 4, they organised a Peer Assist meeting with their suppliers to address the priorities from the self-assessment. One of the supplier representatives who attended that meeting was heard to comment 'It's good to get together, but I feel completely out of my depth here – I'm in a group with managing directors of other companies.' Lord Browne's principle of knowledge-sharing in hierarchies not only applies inside organisations, but also between them.

3. It relies on reciprocity.

People are far more likely to give their time in response to the need of another individual, as we can all identify with times when we have given and received help from others.

In their 1966 Motown hit, 'You can't hurry love', Diana Ross and the Supremes waxed lyrical regarding the 'give and take' nature of love.

This is true of a Peer Assist. This particular technique for learning from experience is also not something which can be hurried, and it relies on the principle of give and take. Someone has to make the first move, and make the request, but if I attend a Peer Assist to offer my experience, I'm more likely to request one in the future. Organisational Karma. Additionally, a Peer Assist is never a one-way experience. Even if I have been invited in to help a colleague by sharing my story, through the dialogue and stories from other peers, I will always learn something new myself that I can take back and apply.

4. It gives voice to experience.

There is a world of difference between sharing opinion and sharing experience. A random tour of the blogo-sphere will illustrate this powerfully. Some blogs are personal experiences, described with colour and depth. They cannot be disputed, because the insights shared are the reflections of an individual, based on something that happened to them, or somewhere they visited. In contrast, other blogs bristle with opinion, beliefs, rants and judgements. These conse-quently attract comment, discussion, debate – and occasionally, abuse! Both types of blogs make for interesting reading, but an ideal Peer Assist is closer to the first type described.

There are plenty of meetings where opinions and beliefs can be shared, but a Peer Assist is not one of them. Opinion is not required at a Peer Assist. However, experience is prized. The core task of anyone facilitating a Peer Assist is to ensure that all of the experience in the room is voiced and listened to. Everyone has something to share and everyone has something to learn.

How a Peer Assist Meeting Works

Peer Assists don't necessarily have to follow a formal meeting structure, provided the principles above are followed. However, we have found the following steps to be helpful for facilitating a planned Peer Assist.

1. The person seeking the assistance (the 'assistee') shares what they know about the problem or issue.

2. The visitors each share their own experiences, stories of what they did in similar or related situations. It is important to coach them to hold back from offering opinions – 'I think you should try x ...'. Instead, the input at this stage should begin – 'When I was in situation y, this is what I experienced ...'.

3. When all of the visitors have had an opportunity to share their stories, the group reflects on the common messages and themes, the things that they all now know, as a result of the preceding exchange.

4. From this common understanding, the group of visitors (with, or without the 'assistee' present) discusses a set of options and possibilities, and presents them back to the 'home team', who can then decide what actions they want to take.

A simple and light-hearted animation which describes the above steps has been developed by internation-

development organisation Bellanet and the University of Ottowa. A copy can be downloaded from www.nomoreconsultants.org.

Let's look at an example of sharing with and learning from peers from Thailand where rice farmers have improved their health, wealth and happiness.

Story 8 – Organic Rice Farming in Thailand

The educational establishments of Thailand recognise that the focus of education so far has been on classroom teaching and training, with teachers serving as 'the font of all knowledge'. They are moving towards action learning, or learning from real life, which is more natural, encourages higher achievement and instils the learning culture among learners and teachers. In action learning, the teacher is no longer an instructor or a knowledgeable person, but becomes a facilitator, an inspirer and a stimulator for learning. Action learning happens by applying the principles and methods of knowledge management.

Here's an example from the Khao Kwan Foundation (KKF) in Suphan Buri Province. The Foundation is applying knowledge management techniques at schools for farmers with great success. The name of the Foundation, 'Khao Kwan' means 'Holy Rice' and the Foundation aims to produce organic rice while reducing the cost of paddy farming and reducing health and environmental hazards.

The students attend one of four schools with typically 40 students to a class, All are practising farmers who have very limited formal education, with their own paddy fields, and are aged from more than 70 years to just over 10 years. How's that for life-long learning? They regularly spend half a day each week for about 16 weeks knowledge-sharing with their peers. Sixteen weeks is a typical cycle time for growing a crop, Over the course of 18 months they grow four crops and can apply their learning immediately to the next crop to 'learn from doing'.

The students at the farming school 'wear two hats', serving as both students and teachers; they do this by rotating the role of teacher amongst themselves. The curriculum is highly flexible since it is designed by the students themselves, with the assistance of KKF knowledge facilitators. They focus on three main practices: pest management without the use of insecticides, soil management without using chemical fertilizers and seed management. The meeting venue is also rotated, sometimes at the local Buddhist temple, and sometimes at a student's home.

Theoretical knowledge is gained from lecturers at the Khao Kwan Foundation and from visiting specialists. These lectures are complemented with study visits – trips to the forest for collecting microbic specimens for soil fertilization, for example. However, the heart of the learning is through self-study on the students' own farms, learning by doing. This is based on observation and note-taking (conditions of the rice stalks, insects, water, soil, living organisms in the field, etc.)

The students use a learning process based on Peer Assist Some have constructed a self-assessment framework arour the practices of pest management, soil management and seed management. Based on each other's strengths they arrange knowledge-sharing study trips to visit those in different districts and take turns in serving as host and guest. Such activity is useful to allow the knowledge gathered to be summarised for sharing more widely and to stimulate new concepts to be tested.

Eighty per cent of the insects indigenous to the Thai Rice fields have a positive impact on the crop, but 20% are destructive. Current insecticides don't discriminate between 'good' and 'bad' insects, so the Thai farmers are pooling their knowledge and experience. They catch samples of the good, the bad and the ugly and identify them. They then learn about the habits and life cycle of each kind of insect, and learn how to check and manage their paddy fields to achieve an insect balance without using insecticide. Specifically, these students learn how to use herbs for insect repellent from a combination of textbooks and local knowledge. They experiment with making their own insect repellent. After a few crops they achieve measurable improvement: higher yield at lower cost, which gives them more income with less work. They are in much better health (more than 90% of their illnesses disappear), they spend less time in the field and have more time for leisure, chatting with their neighbours, and now they can organize community cultural events together like in the old days. They find pleasure and pride in knowledge-sharing and although the plan was for the school to run for one and a half years, after two years the students want to continue learning with some farmers acting as learning facilitators.

(Thanks to Professor Vicharn Panich, The Knowledge Management Institute (KMI), Thailand for this story.)

What do you do when you feel that you have exhausted the opportunities to learn from others within your organisation? Where do you turn to? If you cast an eye in the direction of the River Diagram, this is a situation where the learning comes from the 'north bank' – the bank which describes a level of capability which nobody inside your organisation has yet attained. This is an opportunity to look beyond the boundaries of the organisation, even outside of its sector or industry for the participants in your Peer Assist. It's time to climb up out of the river and seek out the friendly natives who inhabit this Promised Land!

Story 9 – Peers in Unexpected Places – When Great Ormond Street Hospital Met Ferrari!

Great Ormond Street Hospital (GOS) in London is one of the world's leading children's hospitals, with an enviable reputation for pioneering surgical approaches and excellent patient care. Within this environment of excellence and professionalism, there is still a quest for new improvement techniques, a restlessness and frustration borne of a professional desire to 'get it right every time'.

Professor Martin Elliott, who is now Chair of Cardio-Thoracic Services at Great Ormond Street, recounts a fascinating story of how they discovered invaluable life-saving learning in a surprising place. Professor Elliot takes up the story:

It all started with some work done by Professor Marc de Leval at GOS and Professor James Reason from Manchester University. They had been looking at the patient and team risks associated with a procedure which we are all familiar with in our work here – it's known as the arterial switch.

Professor de Leval had become convinced that the successful outcome of an operation involving this procedure was actually more associated with the team or the people involved, than what was wrong with the patient. By an enormous force of will and good management, he persuaded every cardiothoracic surgeon in the country to allow a psychologist to watch their operation and to make notes, record the outcomes and test his hypothesis. And he was right!

In fact, it was the journey to the intensive care unit (ICU) from the operating room, a journey of a few minutes, which was one of the highest risk components of the procedure:

There are a number of reasons for this, but the major one is that the surgeon, supported by his or her team, has spent 6-7 hours looking after a tiny baby in the operating room. When you do this, you really get to know how that baby works – how it responds to drugs, doses of fluid and units of blood. By the end of the operation, you are actually pretty knackered, and you want to move the child to intensive care where a whole other team will pick up the baton. This new team will make sure that the child is safely connected to all the monitoring equipment, and they will closely observe the child for the critical next few hours and beyond.

To make this happen though, you have to disconnect the baby from all the stable monitoring it's on – the drips, the syringe pumps which deliver fluids at a particular rate, the ventilator which has been set to certain settings, the temperature and so on … You have to lift the child out from this nice warm environment, shove it onto a bed, hand-ventilate it down the cold corridor to the ICU and then reconnect it and then pass the information over!

Very sick children are detached from one set of life saving equipment – tubes, wires, monitors, plugs – and connected up to another set before starting their journey to the ICU, administering life preserving drugs en route.

There's a whole series of things going on: a physical transfer, exhausted team handing over to a team that doesn't really want to be there in the evening anyway, and a baby in the middle of all this which has had a life-threatening cardiac operation – and for whom the first 12 hours are also life-threatening. In effect, you are shifting a baby along a chain through a particularly vulnerable moment at a time when both teams are unprepared.

That's the background to the story. Professor Elliott continues:

We'd been operating all night on a Saturday, and completed another operation on the Sunday morning. We were exhausted – and switched on the television. There was the Grand Prix – the perfect thing when you're tired, just sitting gazing at it … suddenly there was a pit stop. It was the McLaren car, 6.8 seconds. As we watched, we were struck with the thought – 'this looks exactly the same as what we do!' It's a high-risk event – a life-threatening event. The car goes into the pits where a huge amount of information is transferred from one team to another team, half of it electronically, some of it verbally over the radio. There are all these people with jobs to do who come in, do stuff, go away and the car goes away very quickly.

It looked a lot better than the way we did it, so we rang them up!

His colleague Allan Goldman, who is the clinical lead in cardiac intensive care, telephoned Bernie Ecclestone who put them in touch with Ferrari. They visited the Ferrari head office in Modena, Italy and met with the then Ferrari chief Jan Todt, the technical race director, Nigel Stepney and technical expert Ross Brawn. They invited them back to Great Ormond Street Hospital.

Surprisingly, we were turned on by all these fast red cars going by, and they were turned on by these tiny little babies that we were operating on. So suddenly there was a meshing of excitement about what we did, and professional interest in watching two teams doing something well, and both of them recognising the problem.

Firstly we started talking about the project, and looking at some early process mapping. For example, their process for changing a tyre was one side of A4. Our equivalent process was fourteen sides of A3! They used video in ways we didn't in the Health Service. They put video cameras up high in the operating theatre similar to where they would normally put video cameras over a pit stop. They did that here with us, and we went out to Maranello to watch them rehearse and do pit stops.

The team at GOS learned most from three main elements of the process which were psychologically and culturally very different. They are to do with communication, the roles of people and the concept of rehearsal.

In the pit stop the driver has to communicate with the team and transfer information to them about the performance of the car so they can do their task effectively. After a five or six-hour operation involving intense concentration, all the doctors want to do is talk to someone to release the tension. As a result of what they have learned they now have a disciplined team briefing so the new team know what happened during the operation, what the patient's vital statistics are – blood pressure, heart rate etc. – and what drugs have been administered and are needed. Everyone hears the same briefing and all have the opportunity to add their relevant information.

On the topic of roles: 'In the NHS, we are all trained to help', says Professor Elliott:

> If someone has a cardiac arrest, the entire intensive care unit rushes towards them, with a trolley usually! People start doing things to the patient who is having a cardiac

arrest, all with a good intent and purpose. With any luck, the baby or adult survives this whole process … If it happens in the street, and you don't know the other people helping, and even more people rush to the person, you can't actually guarantee that they will do the right thing in the right way. So we're trained to help, but there is an instinctive ability to get in each other's way!

As we watched the pit stops in Maranello, we noticed that there were very much clearer definitions of individual roles and responsibilities and leadership over the process. Everyone knows exactly what part they play – changing the left rear wheel, handling the refuelling hose, the stop/go sign, raising and lowering the car with the hydraulic jack.

And on the subject of rehearsals, he says:

The Ferrari team had a much more aggressive pre-event rehearsal. It was a round table exercise where they would walk through every aspect of the pit stop:

'What are we going to do in order to change a tyre?' Car comes in, well, here's the tyre – have I got the tyre ready? Is it the correct tyre? – The left tyre, the right tyre? (There were many instances they could recall where that was not the case!) Is the guy there with the jack? Have I got a nut to put on the wheel? What happens if I haven't got one? They step through all the obvious things like that, and then mentally rehearse the process – who is doing what? Rehearse, rehearse, and then rehearse again – all verbally. Then they go around the table again, asking 'what could go wrong', and 'what would you do if it did go wrong'. All of this happens verbally, deliberately, around the table with someone quietly taking notes. If they can get it perfect in the calmness of the round table, then they stand a good chance of getting it perfect in the deafening, frenetic environment of a Grand Prix circuit.

We don't do any rehearsal in the health service as a convention. We learn from what went wrong rather well, and we do audit, or have a risk team that will come in and look at your event through root cause analysis; but that's all very post-hoc. What Ferrari are doing, both intellectually, and as a company is anticipating much more aggressively what might go wrong, and what they would do about it. Why? Because milliseconds will make a huge financial impact to that racing team.

That rehearsal step then transfers into the real world. They write down protocols that contribute to real processes, keep the protocols on the shelf and focus everything on making them work. They test it with a stopwatch, and hold more rehearsals – eventually with the car and driver present. They want to see who's doing well, what needs to improve, and they repeat it over and over again until the team can do it perfectly every time.

'I can't remember the last time I saw a team in the health service rehearse anything', reflects Professor Elliott. 'More to the point, when are they given time to rehearse anything?'

Back in the hospital, they worked with a human factors expert, Ken Catchpole, who helped them to convert the concepts into something closer to science. He studied what they did, made interventions, and helped create a structured handover with more accurate choreography and clearly allocated tasks. They rehearsed repeatedly and held post-hoc events to analyse and improve on it.

The patient would come in. Firstly there is a defined leader (the anaesthetist at that point) – he looks after the patient. He doesn't do anything or say anything at this point. The Operating Department nurse who manages all the equipment connects the patient up, silently; then that job is done. The nurse puts in the urine catheter and ensures that the drain is on suction, in silence. Those things have to be done to make sure that the baby is safe. The anaesthetist concentrates on the ventilator to make sure the baby is safe. Everyone is silent.

Then, and only then, the handover takes place with the anaesthetist who is in charge with a checklist. The intensivist has an identical checklist – they will be in charge when the handover is complete. They fill these in and acknowledge the receipt of the information. The surgeon is at the back, but is called in when the anaesthesia part is complete, to say what the operation was, what was done, what the risks are. Then the combined anaesthetic, surgical and intensive care team will predict what the outcome is likely to be over the next few hours, and have an outline indication of speed of recovery. At that point the handover is complete and the anaesthetist, the operating department nursing staff, all the people from the operating room and the surgeon can all go. Their work is done – the intensivist is in charge.

All this has taken less time, the number of errors has halved – the mechanical and communication errors have gone down, so the combined error rate has improved even more dramatically. The life of a child has probably been saved.

The cultural rub-off for the Health Service has been that we recognise the value of a bit more discipline around things and the need to improve handover at all levels in the organisation. This will be true for all handovers in every area of healthcare where we don't have continuity, if our patients are going to be safe. We don't have a structure for this – it will have to be a learned behaviour for groups who haven't done it before. I'm optimistic that we will find one – we have to.

So what has Professor Elliott learned from this experience of learning from others?

It pays to be curious. It pays to be aware of what's going on in other areas and not being afraid to ask – I'm proud of my colleague Allan for his perseverance. Complacency is dangerous – there is always room to improve, and there is always someone that you can learn from.

Barriers to Sharing

But not everyone is so open to sharing and learning as these examples. Let's explore some of the 'sharing syndromes' which can beset organisations, and block the flow of learning.

Tall Poppy Syndrome

According to Wikipedia, the origins of this expression comes from Titus Livius' *History of Rome*, in which Lucius Tarquinius Superbus, received a messenger from his son Sextus asking what he should do next in Gabii, since he had become all-powerful there. Rather than answering the messenger, Tarquinius went into his garden, took a stick, and symbolically swept it across his garden, thus cutting off the heads of the tallest poppies that were growing there. The messenger, tired of waiting for an answer, returned to Gabii and told Sextus what happened, who realised that his father wished him to put to death all the most eminent people of Gabii, which he then did.

Thankfully the provenance of the phrase is more extreme than its modern-day parallel! However, the politics in some organisations can generate a culture in which people are reluctant to offer up good practices because they are afraid of the personal cost.

'If I offer a good practice, I am putting myself on a pedestal – ready to be knocked down by others.'

'I don't want to have to endure the scrutiny of my colleagues, picking holes in what I do, giving me all the reasons why my good practice isn't good after all.'

But what if my proposed good practice is genuinely good, and successfully runs the gauntlet of peer scrutiny? What is my reward for such high-quality sharing?

'I'll have to respond to lots of calls, requests and visits if people think I've got something special – I don't have time!'

All three of these assumptions lead to the resulting behaviour: 'Let's just keep our heads down – we're too busy for this.'

Shrinking Violet Syndrome

This is a more subtle syndrome – a form of unmerited corporate humility. Sufferers from shrinking violet syndrome are blissfully unaware that they have anything to share, hence their good practices remain undiscovered by the wider organisation. Sufferers might be heard to say:

'Oh, we're not doing anything special around here.'

'Actually, I'm not sure that anyone ever told us what "good practice" is. We're just doing it the way we always have ...'

'Let's leave it to the experts/head office/policy makers to tell us what we should do.'

In BP, we found that the geographically remote business units were more likely to suffer from shrinking violet syndrome. The Kwinana refinery in Australia had some distinctive ways of working which had remained undiscovered, and hence unshared for many years before the introduction of the Operations Excellence programme.

Tall Poppy and Shrinking Violet syndromes suppress the supply side for sharing knowledge – they prevent people from offering good practices. Let's take a look at two syndromes which affect the demand side.

Not Invented Here Syndrome

No doubt you will have heard of this one, even if you didn't invent it yourself! Not Invented Here (NIH) syndrome is typically embodied by comments such as:

'Ah, you don't understand – we're different here, we couldn't possibly learn from you.'

'We have our own unique culture with unique problems.'

'You'd have to work here for a long time to really understand how things work here.'

This particular syndrome is particularly rife in organisations rich in technical experts, for example, companies with a strong engineering or research culture.

Victor Newman, former Chief Learning Officer at Pfizer, has developed the thinking around 'Not Invented Here' further, suggesting three tips for working with experts suffering from such a syndrome.

Firstly, don't think about presenting the idea using vocabulary which is alien to their own – an immediate giveaway.

Secondly, never present a 100% solution to a group of experts – because they will want to feel like they have improved it themselves and owned it. Learn the art of pausing after 70%, and asking for their help.

Finally, with some hard-core NIH sufferers, you might find that it's not only the content that you share which causes defences to rise but the facilitation method you use to introduce it. 'Hexagonal post-its? Oh, we don't do those!'

When CEO A.G. Lafley started at Procter & Gamble he recognised that to achieve organic growth he needed to seek big ideas from both inside and outside the company. That meant shifting from a 'Not Invented Here' culture. Today more than half of their innovation includes at least one outside partner; they really have transformed the culture.

Our experience is that 'Not Invented Here' syndrome is often underpinned by a problem-solving mindset, or a pioneering spirit, perhaps best summarised as: 'Not only do we have unique problems, we quite like coming up with unique answers!'

The leader of one of BP's business units introduced an informal recognition programme to encourage its members to look beyond the boundaries of their own unit for good practices to adapt and adopt. Entitled 'Steal with Pride', the award took up a pirate theme and was manifested as a cuddly parrot.

If anyone could demonstrate that they had 'stolen' an idea from another business unit, applied it and created value, they would be eligible for the award. The parrot would then take pride of place on their desk for a month, before moving on to the next person. In moving on, the parrot would leave behind a deposit – a solid gold doubloon worth US$ 250. So, for an annual investment of US$ 3000, that business unit leader had sent a powerful message about the importance of learning and adapting, rather than inventing.

An administrative member of staff took up the role of maintaining an intranet-based register of the ideas which had been 'stolen', and the benefits that they had brought to that business unit. This gave visibility and credibility to their approach, and kept staff aware of the benefits of looking outside for learning.

(The unfortunate irony was that none of BP's other business units copied the idea – they didn't invent it!)

Real Men Don't Ask for Directions

The final syndrome to explore here, we have entitled 'Real men don't ask for directions', or for those of you who have an in-car satellite navigation system, 'TomTom Syndrome'!

TomTom syndrome, which seems to affect men more than women, can be diagnosed from comments such as:

'If I ask for help, my colleagues will think I'm incompetent!'

'I didn't get where I am today by admitting weaknesses.'

'In this organisation, the successful ones are the ones who have been self-sufficient.'

'... but, since I'm a good corporate citizen, I'll be happy to share my problem once I've solved it.'

These last two syndromes impact the demand for knowledge – whether through an absence of curiosity, arrogant self-belief or a fear of the consequences of appearing vulnerable. With syndromes like this at work in our organisations, it's a wonder anything ever gets shared!

Using the process of self-assessment can help to address the syndromes above, though not eradicate them. If everyone has used the same assessment tool, with the same descriptions, at a similar point in the year, then some of the 'we're different here' aspects of NIH are neutralised. The transparency of the River Diagram helps to tease out the shrinking violets who can no longer honestly claim 'we didn't know that we were doing anything special', as they sit at the upper reaches of the river, nestling under the north bank.

Using devices such as the Stairs Diagram, Offers and Requests, and the Peer Assist process all help stimulate the exchange, and offer some creative ways to combat the sharing syndromes.

With the summing up of Professor Elliot ringing in our ears,

'It pays to be curious. It pays to be aware of what's going on in other areas and not being afraid to ask ... Complacency is dangerous – there is always room to improve, and there is always someone that you can learn from,' we'll end this chapter and prepare for the next stepping-stone across the river. How do we avoid the dangers of complacency which Professor Elliott described? In the next chapter we look at ways to sustain the process and to develop and improve the self-assessment.

Improving and Sustaining

8

Measuring Progress

The River Diagram works well as a management dashboard, as it throws a spotlight on collective areas of strength and weakness, as well as highlighting the opportunities for knowledge-sharing. If the self-assessment is repeated at regular intervals (every six or 12 months, for example), it should be possible to compare the shape of the river at each stage. You might even create an animation to show how the river is evolving and (hopefully) moving in the right direction.

In principle, if the organisation is learning and improving, the river should gradually 'erode' the north bank (as more business units break through into higher performance), and 'lay up sediment' on the south bank (as more business units improve their performance from a low score). Overall, the width of the river should diminish, as more knowledge-sharing and learning takes place between business units. Sometimes however staff turnover, reorganisations and mergers can disrupt this improvement. In fact the River Diagram could illustrate the disruption caused by such change.

Demonstrating that the organisation is moving forward and increasing its capability against the self-assessment practices can be useful. When supported by stories and examples of improvement, credibility in the approach is built. However, how do the measures of capability on a self-assessment framework relate to other mechanisms for measuring performance in organisations?

Leading and Lagging Indicators

Throughout this book, we have emphasised that the measures in a self-assessment tool focus on leading indicators (input measures) – the things that a team or department need to have in place in order to be successful.

People with responsibility for performance management and improvement will also have a number of lagging indicators (output measures) and Key Performance indicators (KPIs) which they monitor closely.

There may be times where a department scores highly on a leading indicator – i.e. they can demonstrate that they have right capability in place – yet for some reason, the lagging indicator shows a poor performance. This can lead to confusion, and even derision of the self-assessment process. 'How can you claim to have high capability at x when you missed your targets this year?'

In BP, the diagram in Figure 8.1 was used successfully to defuse the tension between proponents of leading and lagging indicators, showing the intervention required in each case.

In areas where leading and lagging indicators are both positive, the management action is 'Celebrate and share the success'.

In areas where the leading indicators are positive, but the lagging indicators are negative, the management action is 'Coach'. It may be that there is a time delay between implementing a capability improvement, and seeing the results impact the output KPIs.

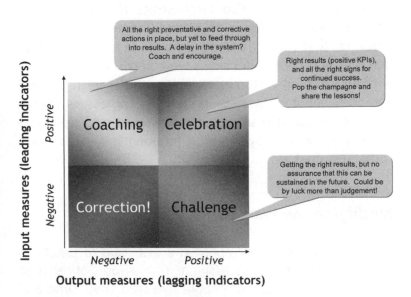

Figure 8.1 Leading and lagging indicators.

In areas where the leading indicators are negative, but the lagging indicators are positive, the management action is 'Challenge'. Perhaps the successful output was attributable to some other factor? How could that business unit give confidence to the organisation that they could repeat the success?

Finally, in areas where both leading and lagging indicators are negative, then the management action must be to 'Correct'.

Let's revisit our 'Effective Meetings' example for the last time. You might imagine that the group were comfortable that their meetings now led to improved decisions which were implemented on time. This was their output measure, or lagging indicator. Using the self-assessment framework, they can also demonstrate that the purpose and desired outcome was always agreed before the meeting, that the pre-circulated agenda included these, and that actions and decisions were recorded and shared with all affected within one week of the meeting. These are their input measures, or leading indicators. Taken together, these two sets of measures can provide assurance that the improvement in meeting quality is likely to be sustainable.

Modifying the Framework

There is nothing sacred about the selection of practices and levels in the self-assessment framework, other than the fact that a group of people invested their time and effort in prioritising and defining them. The practices and levels provide a framework and a common language to enable dialogue and sharing of 'what works'. What is important is that the people using the self-assessment agree on the practices and levels. Perhaps having applied it for a year, you collectively decide that other practices are now more relevant. The world changes and it is important that a self-assessment framework encourages conversations about today's reality rather than reminiscences over yesterday's history. Had we developed a self-assessment framework on 'banking excellence' prior to 2008, would it have looked different to the self-assessment models being developed today?

Even if the practices remain the same, it is possible that good practices and new innovations have pushed the boundaries of level five further out, and that the definitions of these levels should be re-calibrated. That is what continuous improvement is all about!

We suggest that you pause and give some thought to how much you modify it in one year, as radical changes to the self-assessment will make it impossible to compare and measure progress year by year. The ability to measure progress is valuable, as it convinces people that it is a worthwhile approach to persist with, and enables them to link progress against the self-assessment measures with their own personal performance targets.

Local Customisation

Inevitably people will suggest amendments and additional practices to the self-assessment, sometimes before they have tried the process. As a rule of thumb we try to restrict changes to no more than 20%. If possible, agree to collect and acknowledge them throughout the year as people make the suggestions. Continuous improvement doesn't necessarily have to generate continuous change to the self-assessment; you don't want to jeopardise the sharing and learning because the 'common language' which one group have learned has evolved quickly to mean something different.

People may feel that their own department or organisation or region is different; we described this earlier as the 'Not Invented Here' syndrome. Wherever possible, resist local customisation of the entire self-assessment. As a compromise, encourage the use of a core set of common practices which can be shared globally and offer the chance to add two further practices which can be used for their local sharing. Having that option is usually sufficient to overcome the resistance to getting started. Once a group has used the tool, people frequently appreciate that what is different is the action they decide to take rather than the practices or the levels.

External Benchmarking – Towards Level Six

In BP's Operational Excellence programme, there was pressure from the leadership team to continue to push for improved performance. When some groups had reached level five in a particular practice we brought them together to reflect on the question: 'Who are the real leaders in this practice externally, regardless of industry or sector?'

We contacted those leading organisations and asked for help. We shared our approach and asked if they could complete the Operational Excellence self-assessment for that practice. If they felt there was a level six above our own level five, we asked them to suggest some words for it and an example of where it was occurring. This enabled us to keep 'raising the bar' and avoid complacency. Just like Professor Elliott and Ferrari, it pays to be curious and look for your practices in a different context. Ask yourself 'Who is best in the world at this?', and ask them to help you improve. You might be surprised at their responsiveness and the insights that they generate for you.

The self-assessment tool works well to get you on the learning cycle, to establish the routine of plan-do-check-act. Some groups find that using the self-assessment at regular intervals is a good way to sustain the momentum, while others, having got into the cycle of learning, focus on regular learning and sharing in all of their activities.

Let us look at an example from Latin America where the approach has been in use for more than five years.

Story 10 – The Sustainable Development of Cities

The UN has determined that, for the first time in history, the majority of people worldwide are now living in cities. Of all continents, Latin America has the highest percentage of urban population and at the same time faces the challenges of lack of financial resources and political instability. Recognising this trend, the UN Institute for Training and Research (UNITAR) has created a Decentralised Cooperation programme and in partnership with city councils has set up a network of 12 regional training centres known as CIFAL (a French acronym standing for International Training Centres for Local Authorities and Local Actors). They are hubs for sharing good practice and experience. Many cities are facing similar challenges. Rather than propose a single 'one size fits all' solution, these centres create an environment where local government officials can compare notes with their peers from other cities. One of these centres was established in Curitiba, Brazil in 2003, providing a variety of events promoting the sharing of knowledge on themes relating to sustainable development and provision of public services.

CIFAL Curitiba benefits from having a multi-disciplinary team experienced in group work, adult learning, training and knowledge management. UNITAR has provided the methodology based on sound knowledge management principles, including self-assessment, and called it the 'Cityshare methodology'.

Participants in the learning events find the self-assessment easy to use; it allows self-awareness of capabilities and at the same time demystifies the topics under discussion, since people are sharing real experiences. The CIFAL Curitiba team are well versed in the methods and adapt the self-assessment tool according to the theme of the event. They have built frameworks for integrated waste management, water management, public transport systems and social inclusion policies. For example, at a recent event on Social Inclusion they used a self-assessment with 11 practices to assess, covering diagnosis and resolution of the issues, creating and implementing policies, and managing social inclusion in areas of risk. Typically between 80 and 100 people participate and at the 15 events already carried out 100% of participants rated the event as either very good or good. For example they recently held a regional meeting in Montevideo in Uruguay. A whopping 94% of participants considered that the method added to their knowledge of the topic. One participant commented:

> The method allows us to focus sharing positive experiences on which relevant new policies and processes for social and economic development can be built.

The River Diagram and Stairs Diagram are analysed to form the discussion groups in order to match the exchange of successful experience with assistance requests. These discussion groups are run as Peer Assists after which knowledge assets are built. The method provides the opportunity to bring together 'those who already know how to' with 'those who want to learn'. A key part of their process is action planning and subsequent monitoring of progress. Following the sharing and capturing of knowledge each participating city drafts a 'City Action Plan' which includes indicators of progress.

Some examples of the actions the approach has stimulated are:

- A partnership between Curitiba and Santiago de Los Caballeros in the Dominican Republic, to deal with waste management, public transport and park systems.

- A technical cooperation between Curitiba and San José in Costa Rica to deal with urban planning and transport.

- Technical visits between Curitiba and Medellin and Bogota in Colombia to improve the configuration of transport systems.

A virtual community has been set up in order to build on the events, to sustain the momentum of sharing of experiences and to strengthen the CIFAL network. An e-mail prompts participants to monitor City Action Plans and they share progress, new experiences and items of common interest on the virtual community site. For those who can read Spanish, see www.cifalcuritiba.org.br for details.

The approach is creating synergies between Latin American cities, and by using simple-to-understand tools tailored to local needs they are learning to build sustainable cities together. Or as one Latin American participant at a CIFAL event summarised:

'Metodología muy buena e innovadora'

'A very good and innovative methodology'.

(Thanks to Charlotte Diez of UNITAR for capturing and giving permission to share this experience.)

To summarise the points from this chapter:

- The self-assessment framework does not have to be perfect first time around, but it does need to be agreed upon.

- As people make use of it, improvements will come to mind.

- Record these suggestions but maintain a global standard for a year to give everyone the opportunity to use the same tool.

- Agree amendments, keeping a balance between improvement and comparability.

- By keeping peers connected they can help to monitor progress of action plans.

- By sharing internally, the spread of levels for any one practice should close. Then it is time to look outside to raise the bar.

Looking outside in order to raise the bar brings us back to the question posed by the title of the book. We have explored in depth how we can improve performance by defining the issue and learning from ourselves first, and then by learning from other organisations.

So is that it? What do we do now? And with all these new avenues in which to seek improvement, where and how *do* consultants fit in?

So What Do We Do Now?

9

Throughout this book we have been developing the idea that if we know what our organisations are good at, and where that good practice can be found, then we may not need to look to a consultant to resolve our issues for us. It is also true that, if we can get clear about exactly why we need a consultant, then we are more likely to hire the right one.

This chapter returns to the topic of the use of consultants. The techniques described in the preceding chapters go a long way towards creating an intelligent, sharing and learning culture. A culture in which the low-hanging fruits often collected by eager consultants have long since been consumed by the organisation which has produced them.

Of course, we are not claiming that every organisation can do without consultants completely; however, it can be more purposeful in why it is using them and whom it selects. Not all consultants live up to their reputation for 'borrowing your wristwatch to tell you the time'. There are plenty who will help you to discover the value of a discarded watch, or show you how to wind and maintain your timepiece to sustain its use. This is a good thing, provided your watch is the real issue at hand.

The subtitle of the book is 'We know more than we think'. This chapter places a comma into the phrase to suggest that 'we know, more than we think', and entreats you to invest more time thinking more about the purpose, timing and selection of consultants. That way, you will unleash the value latent within your organisation, and invest wisely in the right consultants at the most appropriate time.

By changing your outlook to appreciate strengths rather than looking for and solving problems, you are likely to recognise the competencies within the organisation. If you know what the organisation knows, then you can make good use of that and also work on the areas you need to improve. By the time you have reached this chapter of the book you'll already be confident about how best to know the strengths of your organisation and how to deal with the shortcomings.

You can conduct the right conversations and develop a shared understanding of the issue to be resolved. By holding a meeting to create a self-assessment framework, and then using the framework to have a conversation to elicit strengths and gaps, you'll be well positioned to know what you need to learn.

If you know what knowledge you need, or which practices you need to improve, then you can seek out the people who have experience to share inside and outside the organisation, and who can help you fill the gaps. You can then deal with the issue by learning from the experiences of others and then collaborating with them to build on those experiences. If you repeat the process after an interval then you can measure your improvement. This is the key to sustainable performance.

If at any of the above stages you feel that you do not have the necessary competence, resources or ability then you might well consider bringing in help from outside, often in the form of a consultant. It is worth taking a step back and thinking about the situation. As a potential customer, what exactly do you want from the consultant? You might need help in defining or more closely diagnosing the underlying issue, in coming up with solutions and options to deal with the issue, and in implementing the resulting change; or perhaps a combination of all three.

During the writing of this book, we have been challenged by consulting colleagues to explain where we think consultants should play a role, and the thought process an organisation should go through in order to make those decisions. In the pages which follow, we have endeavoured to do just that.

In Chapter 1 we posed five key questions:

- Can we identify the issue?

- Do we know our internal capability?

- Does anyone do this well internally?

- If not, do we know who is good at it externally?

- Having identified who does it well, are they available to help us, either by sharing what they know or by implementing it?

We can visualise this now as a process flow diagram (Figure 9.1) which takes you from diagnosing the issue, to solving the issue and finally implementing the solution.

Can We Identify the Issue?

Time invested understanding the underlying issue, the root cause, rather than jumping to treat the symptom is time well spent. Having 'fresh eyes' to look at what is going on can avoid myopia. You may already be clear what the issue is that you wish to deal with or you might consider getting help to identify the issue.

Do We Know Our Internal Capability?

The self-assessment approach allows you to identify the capabilities of the organisation in order to deal with the issue, and where the strengths lie in the organisation. The River Diagram enables you to visualise that distribution of strengths. The self-assessment approach creates a conversation amongst the right people to enable sharing and learning.

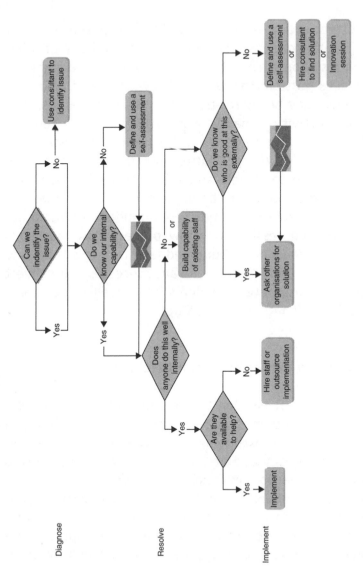

Figure 9.1 Diagnose, resolve and implement.

Does Anyone Do this Well?

Too often we look only at the current competencies being used in the organisation and we are ignorant of what strengths people have that are available to the organisation. It is possible that all the knowledge and resources you need may be there, but since this is not a business-as-usual activity, it may be worth having a coach help the team get to 'match fitness'. The task force assembled from those in the organisation should consist of a wide range of people, levels and roles. This will encourage buy-in to the solution to be implemented, but remember that those people may not feel confident to facilitate brainstorming sessions or draw process flow diagrams. Employing someone to build and facilitate this team and to introduce them to the relevant processes will convert a group of disparate individuals into a well-drilled team capable of lifting the World Cup!

Do We Know Who is Good at it Externally?

If we know that we don't have the capability in-house, then who does possess the key knowledge that we could reach out to? By extending our social networks further, we might identify and be able to approach 'people who know' in other organisations. Perhaps Ferrari have a Formula 1 Facebook group! Self-assessment across organisations may identify the different strengths and provide a basis for reciprocal sharing. People do feel appreciated for their strengths, and it gives them a sense of pride to be helping others. Even if we have the capability in-house it may be beneficial to also look externally for new ideas to stimulate innovation.

Are the People with the Knowledge Available to Help Us?

We may have the capability and know-how, or have learned it from others, yet we may still need additional people to help implement the solution. In which case do we need to hire staff on a permanent basis or do we just want to outsource this particular task?

If the knowledge lies outside the organisation will they be prepared to assist us? Do we have an existing relationship? Is there something we can offer that they need, to reciprocate the help? Or is this a conversation we can both benefit from? All these are good questions to ask, to prepare the ground for making a request for help.

We hope that working through these decision points with a real business issue in mind will bring to life the message of 'No More Consultants'.

We set out to share something which we have seen work in a variety of organisations and settings; from international oil companies to the fight against HIV/AIDS, from the optimisation of a supply chain to the creation of inter-company networks. It's a simple, structured process for engaging people in dialogue about the relative strengths and weaknesses, and the variations across the organisation, whilst avoiding egos and side-stepping internal competition.

We hope that we have also shown you how the journey can be one which can be involving, creative and energising for your staff, giving them a sense that their knowledge and experience is truly valued. Together they build the stepping stones to get to the other bank of the river.

We are confident that it will ensure you are in better shape to use consultants wisely.

Because you know more than you think.

Appendix

A

Self-Assessment Framework for Effective Meetings

	Design the meeting	Prepare and Share Relevant Material	Get the Right People into the Meeting
Level 5 Lifestyle	We always prepare well for our meetings and only hold one if the purpose and outcomes are clearly defined. Meeting rooms are equipped with technology to enable virtual participation.	We always allocate agenda items and digest relevant pre-read so that the meeting time can be used for discussing and agreeing. We read material so we are well prepared for the topic.	We invite customers and those affected to hear their viewpoint. We get knowledgeable people and a few 'wildcards' to get diverse viewpoints to enrich the discussion.
Level 4 Scale	We plan each meeting to achieve the purpose, outcomes and deliverables for all our meetings. We use carefully chosen venues which enhance the meeting effectiveness.	We send out an agenda well in advance. We routinely assign agenda items and circulate relevant information beforehand, giving sufficient time for it to be read.	We invite some people who will be affected by our actions and decisions. We invite people who are knowledgeable about the topic but not directly involved.
Level 3 Action	The meeting owner and facilitator agree the purpose, desired outcomes and agenda items. We consider the physical environment, whether the meeting needs to be face-to-face, and whether some or all attendees could be virtual.	We consider what will be useful to share for our agenda item, but only when we are seeking agreement or approval. We read what is circulated before the meeting starts.	We co-opt people with key knowledge to join the meeting for specific agenda items. We give some thought to who might be affected by the decisions.
Level 2 Reaction	When someone asks, we explain the purpose of the meeting and what we'd like to get from it. It's clear whether we are sharing ideas or taking decisions.	Agendas are sent out before the meeting. We distribute some pre-reading a day before the meeting, usually something that already exists.	We invite the project or team members but no one else, unless they request to attend.
Level 1 Basic	We have an agenda, somewhere to meet and an agreed date and time.	We know it is a good idea to circulate pre-reading but we don't always have the time.	We limit the number of people in the meeting to avoid wasting others' time.

Everyone Plays an Active Role	Use Agreed Meeting Processes	Summarise and Share Decisions and Actions
Everyone in the meeting plays an active role – even if that role is simply to listen actively. Roles are rotated from time to time.	Ideas are built upon and new ideas emerge from the group. Everyone is clear about the decision-making process. Recorded agreements and actions are visible to all participants as they are captured. (Flip chart or screen.) Actions are reviewed.	We consider who needs to be aware of decisions and actions agreed, and ensure that they are aware.
We routinely use facilitators to energise the meeting and to make sure sensitive issues get discussed, recorders to capture key agreements and a timekeeper to keep us on track. Virtual participants feel fully involved.	We have a 'Ground Rules for Meetings' document posted in each meeting room. We have a process for participants to revise draft minutes. We review expectations, purpose and outcomes at the start and end of every meeting.	We review agreements and actions at the end of meetings. We have a common space for minutes to be shared.
The meeting has a facilitator who makes sure everyone participates. Where necessary, we assign roles – recorder, timekeeper etc. We stick to agreed time allocation, or renegotiate it, to ensure all agenda items are given sufficient time.	We are clear whether we are brainstorming or reaching closure. We agree a process for arriving at a decision before we need it. We agree ground rules at the start of each meeting. A recorder captures minutes.	We have a template for writing and circulating minutes and actions, with delivery dates and action owners.
Someone chairs the meeting. We'll assume silence means agreement and we limit discussion time. Virtual participants are sometimes ignored or forgotten.	People know when to bring up their point in the agenda. The chair determines how we will make a decision – usually a simple vote. We generally review previous actions and minutes, and sometimes cover the same ground twice.	We write and circulate minutes and actions, often when reminded by someone in time for the next meeting.
We only speak if it is our task or if we have expertise on the agenda item.	People exchange ideas but they are not built upon. 'Let's talk till we all agree, or until one side backs down!' We can't get the technology in the meeting room to work so we manage without it.	We leave it to individuals to note down their own actions.

Appendix

B

Learning and Development
Self-Assessment Framework

	Evaluating Success	Business Alignment
Level 5	The impact of Learning has made a clearly evidenced difference to business performance. Demonstrates a considered balance between quality and cost-effectiveness. Wise choices are made as to the degree and scope of evaluation.	Learning strategy aligned with business strategy and built with/by the business, taking into account medium to long-term future direction. L&D consistently has a direct influence at a senior level on business issues. Everything the L&D function provides is driven by the business. L&D has the authority and the nerve to take tough decisions.
Level 4	Consistently used measures of success in place. Compelling stories of business impact exist. Degree and scope of evaluation is regularly reviewed.	Learning strategy is aligned with current business strategy. Examples exist where L&D has had a direct influence at senior levels of the business. L&D speaks the language of the business and has a 'seat at the table' during business planning – e.g. via 'visionary interviews'.
Level 3	Measures development success in some areas, but not in others (e.g. between parts of the business or in relation to varied programmes). A few measures of success are used, but not consistently.	The L&D Community influences and advises on L&D matters, taking into account immediate/short-term changes. Business cases made for L&D proposals. Partnership between L&D and business is acknowledged.
Level 2	Impact is inferred rather than proven. Evaluation rarely extends beyond the quality of learning and events.	Some planning mechanisms exist between L&D and the business, but the focus is on products and processes. Some evidence of L&D being perceived as a strategic advisor/partner.
Level 1	Measures whether development has made a difference to learners. Judgements made on basic evidence (e.g. anecdotal feedback).	Strategy drawn up within L&D function with limited reference to business and in reaction to change. Basic L&D customer/provider relationship. L&D function makes decisions on provision with limited reference to business.

Supporting a Learning Culture	Providing Development Options
L&D is valued by most staff and managers. All staff take ownership of their learning and development. Leaders use L&D as an integral part of running the business. Learning before and after is seen as integral to professional delivery of business activities.	Business needs are met at the right time, at optimum cost, using the most appropriate delivery mechanism. Thorough understanding of target population and management needs. Robust mechanisms for analysis of needs. Bespoke solutions generated to meet business outcomes.
L&D is appreciated by many staff, and has several senior advocates. Progressive staff take ownership for their learning and development. Some business support for learning before and after activities.	A number of needs analysis methods are in use, and are known to be effective. Tailored solutions are developed where needed. Advisors and on-line guidance available to help selection of appropriate options.
Most people are aware of how L&D can support them. The majority of L&D is available through a variety of delivery channels. Learning before and after significant events will happen when prompted. Some leaders use L&D as an integral part of running the business.	Classroom events are complemented with e-learning and other methods. Some tailored solutions exist. A mechanism for analysing development needs exists and always delivers a learning solution.
L&D seen as key to developing a learning culture. Occasional evidence of 'learning before doing' and 'learning after doing', but this is inconsistently applied.	Classroom events are converted directly to e-learning, rather than re-designed as blended solutions. Mechanisms exist to analyse needs, but these are not always followed effectively.
Relatively small selection of delivery channels used by L&D. Learning culture is embryonic. L&D is not high on the agenda for business leaders.	Traditional prospectus with scheduled classroom delivery as the norm. Limited differentiation of learners' needs and few individual solutions. Product delivery method is driven as much by costs and available skills, as by outcomes.

Managing the L&D Function

Level 5	Strategy exists, fully aligned with business plans, taking into account future direction of the business and L&D innovation. Appropriate professional standards applied. A skilled and flexible workforce with future workforce planning. Lean, robust, fully functioning and regularly reviewed customer-focused systems and processes. Embedded culture of continuous improvement. Robust business and financial planning.
Level 4	L&D Strategy exists and is fully aligned with business strategy. LMS is fully used, well regarded and delivers a clear return on investment. L&D is able to respond and flex as the business climate changes.
Level 3	The L&D delivery plan generally aligns with business and central initiatives. L&D processes encourage/require individuals to undertake their own needs analysis. The L&D function manages its budget effectively and balances its books. An LMS is in place and generally used.
Level 2	LMS is in place, but under-utilised. Resources managed within budget, rather than to optimum organisation-wide effectiveness. Innovative products and delivery are the exception rather than the rule.
Level 1	Basic policies, products and plans in place. Favours tried-and-tested ways of working. Function sometimes struggles to keep pace with business changes. Resource management and budgeting is generally achieved, but tends to be reactive and pressurised. Majority of staff not professionally qualified in L&D.

Influencing Stakeholders	Assuring Professional Delivery
Voice is heard and actively sought, at all levels of the organisation up to and including the most senior levels. Achieves recognition outside the organisation (e.g. wins an award, consulted by external customers for advice). Uses sophisticated and targeted approaches to marketing. Seen as a strategic business partner contributing to the business planning in the organisation.	Mutually supportive relationship with trusted suppliers. Suppliers work together to produce innovative interventions. All material is consistently high-quality and, where appropriate, is leading edge. A culture of continuous review, improvement and piloting exists. All needs of diverse groups are catered for.
Clear understanding and tracking of key stakeholders, regularly reviewed. L&D is viewed increasingly as a strategic function. Marketing capability is available within the function and is used to great effect with stakeholders and customers.	Optimal blend of delivery interventions. Some collaboration and co-creation between suppliers, when prompted. Material is continually improved to ensure consistently high quality.
Various channels of communication are used to promote development options. The profile of the function is established, but tends to be more operational than strategic. Well regarded by many stakeholders. Stakeholder mapping is used to analyse the organisational landscape.	There is a tried and tested quality assurance process in place. All L&D material is quality-assured by technical/professional leads. Good blend of delivery interventions is available. Suppliers are regarded as experts in their fields. Needs of diverse groups are met in part.
Some senior stakeholders are fully engaged, and supportive of strategic L&D. The L&D function is credible with stakeholders, but generally perceived as a deliverer of training solutions.	Diverse groups can be catered for, depending on circumstances and supplier. A preferred supplier list exists, and is used for key products.
Basic communication about development options is undertaken, e.g. distributing advertising. Little access to senior stakeholders. Some credibility within the organisation, but not consistent and widespread. Some success in selling new ideas to the business.	Material is generally pitched at the right audience. Casual/ad hoc relationships with suppliers. Evaluation is undertaken but lessons are not always applied, hence little changes. Basic provision to meet the needs of diverse groups.

Source: Provided by courtesy of the National School of Government.

Appendix C

Creating a River Diagram with Excel

These guidance notes have been written for Excel 2007. Please refer to www.nomoreconsultants.org for more recent versions as they are released.

An Excel Chart Template is freely available on www. nomoreconsultants.org, which will automate the process below. The process is included for those of you who like to think things through from first principles or may wish to adapt it!

A River Diagram is a combination of two Excel chart types, plotted on two axes of the same chart:

- Stacked 2D Area chart: this marks out the boundaries of the River, the highest and lowest scores for each practice.

- Line with markers: this is used to display the curr and target scores.

	A	B	C	D	E	F	G
		practice 1	practice 2	practice 3	practice 4	practice 5	practice 6
1							
2	min	=MIN(B6:B10)	=MIN(C6:C10)	=MIN(D6:D10)	=MIN(E6:E10)	=MIN(F6:F10)	=MIN(G6:G10)
3	spread	=B4-B2	=C4-C2	=D4-D2	=E4-E2	=F4-F2	=G4-G2
4	max	=MAX(B6:B10)	=MAX(C6:C10)	=MAX(D6:D10)	=MAX(E6:E10)	=MAX(F6:F10)	=MAX(G6:G10)
5	Current score						
6	Group 1	1	2	4	3	2	4
7	Group 2	3	2	2	4	1	5
8	Group 3	2	5	3	3	3	3
9	Group 4	2	3	2	3	3	3
10	Group 5	1	2	3	3	2	3
11							
12	Target score						
13	Group 1	3	2	4	3	4	4
14	Group 2	3	3	2	4	3	5
15	Group 3	4	5	3	4	3	3
16	Group 4	4	3	5	3	3	3
17	Group 5	3	3	3	3	2	3

Figure C.1 Spreadsheet.

1. For a simple River Diagram with six practices and five groups participating, create the table below in Excel (Figure C.1).

   min calculates the minimum of the five groups' current scores, **max** calculates the biggest current score and **spread** is the difference between the maximum and minimum.

2. Select the top three rows of the table, and from the menu, select Insert: Area: Stacked Area Chart, which will create the chart below (Figure C.2).

3. Select the y axis, right-click and select 'axis options' and set the Maximum: option to be fixed, with the value 5.

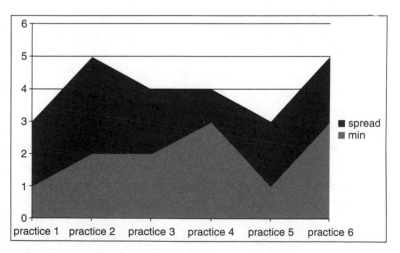

Figure C.2 Shaded area chart.

4. Set the Major unit to be fixed, with value 1. Click OK.

5. Click in the white area above the brown 'gap' series, but not on a gridline. Select Format Plot Area: Solid Fill and choose a green colour. This will be your river bank.

6. Select a grid line, right-click and choose: Format Gridlines. Select Solid Line and choose the same green colour as the river bank, thereby making your gridlines invisible.

7. Click in the solid blue area (the minimum series), right-click and choose Format Data Series. Choose Fill: Solid Fill, and select the same green colour. You now have both river banks defined.

8. Select the brown 'river', and repeat the sequence in 7 above, choosing the blue colour of your choice. You should now have a blue river with green banks (Figure C.3).

   Now to add the current and target scores for one group.

9. Click in the blue river, right-click and chose Select Data. Click Add. Set the Series Name to 'current score', and set the Series values to row containing the current scores of group 1. Click OK.

10. Click Add again, and Select Data. This time Series Name is 'target score' and Series values is set to the

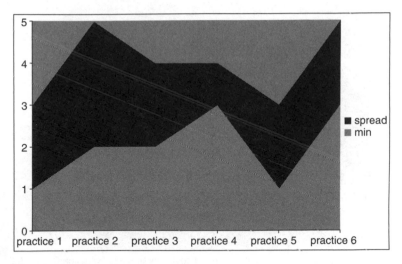

Figure C.3 Blue river.

row with the same group's target scores. Click OK. Your river will have taken on a strange shape, and the north green bank will have been replaced. Don't panic! (Figure C.4).

You now need to change the chart type for the last two series added, so that they appear as lines.

11. Click in the current score series, right-click and select Change Series Chart Type. Select Line with markers. Repeat this for the target score series.

You should now have a strange-looking chart, wi a green surround (Figure C.5). (This is not the c if you are using Excel 2003 so you can skip step

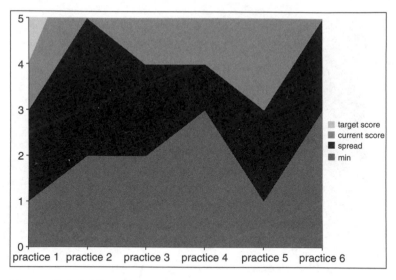

Figure C.4 Adding the scores.

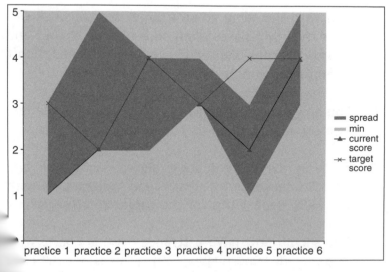

Figure C.5 Line charts.

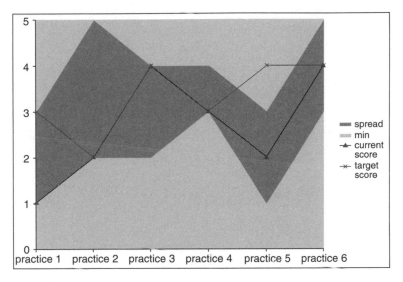

Figure C.6 Final River Diagram.

12. Your final step is to select the x axis, right-click and chose Axis Options. The final option is Position Axis. Choose On tick marks. The green surround will magically disappear, and you will be left with a River Diagram resembling the one below (Figure C.6).

13. You can delete the legend and reformat the axis text, should you choose.

14. You can now copy the River Diagram by right-clicking on the chart tab and repeat steps 9 to 12 for another group's scores. The shape of the river will remain the same.

Appendix D

Knowledge and Organisation Development in the NHS

	1 Concept	2 Reaction
Taking a strategic approach	Isolated people with a passion for knowledge management begin to talk and share how difficult it is to implement.	Most people say sharing know-how is important. People are using some tools to help with capture and sharing.
Leadership	Leaders are sceptical as to the benefits of knowledge-sharing. Knowledge is 'power'.	Some leaders give people the time to share and learn, but there is little visible support.
Building a learning organisation	People are conscious of the need to learn from what they do but rarely get the time.	People capture what they learn on an ad hoc basis but the learning is rarely accessed by others.
Networking	People work on individual objectives alone.	People are networking and collaborating to complete specific tasks, but feel the need to defend the time. Ad hoc Networks/Communities of Practice (CoPs) are created.
Measuring the value	People have faith that sharing knowledge is adding value but cannot demonstrate it.	Anecdotal stories demonstrate benefits. There are some indicators.
Capturing and reapplying knowledge	People are moved on to next work before they have time to learn lessons.	People capture lessons and store them locally. They respond to 'customers' requests for knowledge.
Innovation	Everyone's free to do things their own way. People sometimes innovate when a good solution already exists.	Innovation priorities decided by established company strategy. Good ideas get implemented.
Implementing efficiencies in our working practices	We prefer to do things the way we have always done them.	We recognise the need to change our working practices and are independently looking for efficiencies.

Source: Adapted from the unpublished KM tool, developed by C Collison and G Parcell, co-authors of *Learning to Fly*.

3 Action	4 Scale	5 Lifestyle
Some job descriptions include knowledge capture, sharing and effective usage, linked to KSF core dimensions 2 and 4.[a] There are isolated knowledge projects.	A strategy for knowledge-sharing exists but is not linked to business results. A clear framework and set of tools for work-related learning is widely communicated and understood.	The knowledge-sharing strategy is embedded in the Trust's/SHA's business strategy. A framework and tools enable learning before, during and after.
The organisation recognises that people should share and learn from each other, and that knowledge is everyone's responsibility. However in reality it is left to a small isolated few.	There is a clear signal from the top and leaders across the organisation set an example in sharing and learning from each other.	The right attitudes exist to share and use others' know-how. All leaders reinforce the right behaviour and act as role models.
Common processes are in place for the sharing and reapplying of knowledge.	People are learning before, during and after activities. Peer to peer learning is common.	Communities review and validate learning to improve and revise existing processes.
CoPs are organised around practice areas. They have a clear document which defines purpose, ground rules and membership.	Individuals regularly benefit by networking. Local available IT tools are utilised to locate and share knowledge. Linkages between networks exist.	Networks and CoPs help deliver organisational goals and have become part of the culture.
Qualitative and quantitative indicators are devised, but are only referred to when evaluations are required.	People design, measure and apply improvements continuously to add value.	The effective use of knowledge is acknowledged across the organisation as central to service improvement and improving safer care.
People capture content designed around the organisation's and 'customers' needs, but it is not always accessed.	There is a process that 'pushes' relevant knowledge and contacts to the right people.	'Just in time' knowledge is current and easily accessible throughout the organisation.
Experimentation leads to pilot projects. Priorities clearly linked to responsiveness to customer needs.	Successful experimentation leads to wide rollout. New horizons identified and value quickly created from them.	The organisation reviews and improves innovation processes. Innovation a core competence of most staff.
We are learning from each other about how to be more efficient.	We understand the health needs and concerns of the local population/patients and have processes in place to address them.	Performance comes from continuous improvement of our working practices.

[a] NHS Knowledge and Skills Framework core dimension 2 Personal and People Development and 4 Service Improvement.

Further Reading

Chapter 1

The BP Operations excellence programme was described in Chris Collison and Geoff Parcell, *Learning to Fly – Practical Knowledge Management from Leading and Learning Organizations* (Chichester: John Wiley and Sons Ltd, 2nd edn, 2004).

Donald Rumsfeld was talking to troops in Kuwait about to head into Iraq. reported in the *Washington Post*, December 9, 2004.

Chapter 2

Chris Collison and Geoff Parcell, *Learning to Fly – Practical Knowledge Management from Leading and Learning Organizations* (Chichester: John Wiley and Sons Ltd, 2nd edn, 2004).

Don Tapscott and Anthony D Williams, *Wikinomics* (London: Atlantic Books, 2007).

Chapter 3

Jim Collins, *Good to Great* (London: Random House, 2001).

James Surowiecki, *The Wisdom of Crowds* (London: Abacus, 2004).

Jane Watkins & Bernard Mohr, *Appreciative Inquiry – Change at the Speed of Imagination* (San Francisco: Jossey-Bass/Pfeiffer, 2001).

Positive Deviance was promoted by Jerry and Monique Sternin during their work on child nutrition in Vietnam. It is described in a British Medical Journal article 'The Power of Positive Deviance' by Marsh, Schroeder, Dearden, Sternin and Sternin, November 2004: 329.

For more about OneSixSigma, Six Sigma and Lean see www.onesixsigma.com/.

To learn more about the I&I community see www.improvementand-innovation.com/.

More about the National School of Government can be found at www.nationalschool.gov.uk.

Chapter 4

Peter Senge, *The Fifth Discipline* (London: Century Business, 1992). Chapter 11 discusses Shared Vision.

Bill Jensen, *Simplicity* (Cambridge, MA: Perseus Books, 2001) is about creating simpler organisations through clearer communications.

For more about response to HIV/AIDS see www.aidscompetence.org.

For more about Oracle's professional communities and their 'Guide to Virtual Working' see www.oracle.com/global/eu/corp-commit/download/kmr.pdf.

Government Office for the North West www.gos.gov.uk/gonw/.

Chapter 5

Sam Kaner et al., *The Facilitator's Guide to Participatory Decision Making* (Gabriola Island, BC, Canada: New Society Publishers, 1996).

Chapter 6

For examples of the River Diagram for you to try go to www.nomoreconsultants.org.

The poem, 'Halfway down the stairs' is taken from A A Milne, *The Christopher Robin Story Book* (Dutton, 1957).

Report of a national review of NHS health library services in England: from knowledge to health in the 21st century (2008) Recommendation 11, p. 36 available from: www.library.nhs.uk/nlhdocs/national_library_review_final_report_4feb_081.pdf.

NHS Institute for Innovation and Improvement, *The Role of the Chief Knowledge Officer: In An NHS Organisation V3* (2008): www.library.nhs.uk/nlhdocs/chief_knowledge_officer_paper.doc.

Chapter 7

To learn more about Peer Assist go to Chapter 7 of Chris Collison and Geoff Parcell, *Learning to Fly – Practical Knowledge Management from Leading and Learning Organizations* (Chichester: John Wiley and Sons Ltd, 2nd edn, 2004).

Chapter 8

For more about the UNITAR programme see www.dcp.unitar.org/-CIFAL-Network-.html.

Chapter 9

For resources go to www.nomoreconsultants.org.

Index

*Compiled by Indexing Specialists
(UK) Ltd*